Kingdom of God Series

Studies in the development of the Kingdom of God,
for use consecutively or as independent units.

The Religion of Israel.
Twenty-six lessons.   By John Bayne Ascham.
Teacher's Manual for The Religion of Israel.

The Religion of Judah.
Twenty-six lessons.   By John Bayne Ascham.

The Life of Jesus.
Twenty-six lessons.   By Harris Franklin Rall.
Teacher's Manual for The Life of Jesus.

The Teachings of Jesus.
Twenty-six lessons.   By Harris Franklin Rall.
Teacher's Manual for The Teachings of Jesus.

Apostles, Fathers, and Reformers. By John Bayne Ascham.
Teacher's Manuals. For each unit, ready or in preparation.

Life and Service Series

Short elective courses

Studies in the Parables of Jesus.   By Halford E. Luccock.
Heart Messages from the Psalms.   By Ralph Welles Keeler.
Amos, Prophet of a New Order.   By Lindsay B. Longacre.
Elements of Personal Christianity.   By William S. Mitchell.
The Christian in Social Relationships.
                          By Dorr Frank Diefendorf.
Deuteronomy, a Prophetic Lawbook. By Lindsay B. Longacre.
Christian Ideals in Industry.
                  By F. Ernest Johnson and Arthur E. Holt.

International Graded Series

The Bible and Social Living. Fifty-two lessons. In one
     volume or in quarterly parts. By Harry F. Ward.
The History and Literature of the Hebrew People. Fifty-two
     lessons. In one volume or in quarterly parts. By
     Robert W. Rogers.

LIFE AND SERVICE SERIES

HENRY H. MEYER, Editor
WADE CRAWFORD BARCLAY, Associate Editor

STUDIES IN THE PARABLES OF JESUS

By
HALFORD E. LUCCOCK

Approved by the Committee on Curriculum
of the Board of Sunday Schools of the
Methodist Episcopal Church

THE METHODIST BOOK CONCERN
NEW YORK   CINCINNATI

Copyright, 1917, by
HALFORD E. LUCCOCK

Printed in the United States of America

First Edition Printed November, 1917
Reprinted May, 1918; April, September and November, 1919; August, 1920
August, 1922; January, 1924; April, 1925; October, 1926

CONTENTS

CHAPTER   PAGE

Life and Service Series................... 5

A Word from the Author............... 7

I. The Lost Sheep. The Lost Coin........ 9

II. The Prodigal Son....................... 18

III. The Parable of the Sower............. 28

IV. The Two Foundations................... 37

V. The Pearl of Great Price. The Hidden
Treasure.............................. 45

VI. The Good Samaritan.................... 55

VII. The Ten Virgins........................ 65

VIII. The Unmerciful Servant................ 75

IX. The Talents............................. 85

X. The Pharisee and the Publican......... 95

XI. The Rich Fool........................... 104

XII. The Mustard Seed. The Leaven........ 113

XIII. The Last Judgment..................... 123

CONTENTS

I. My Ancestral Home 1

II. Sheila Takes a Mission 7

III. The Law before The Law Comes 9

IV. Some Personal Notes 15

V. The First Family of the South 23

VI. The Two Plantations 31

VII. The First of Great Price, The Hand of Esther 38

(?) 44

VII. Shiela Tells a Story 62

VIII. The Wonder of a Signal 75

IX. The Tailors 83

X. The Planter and the Tailors 98

XI. The Rose Grove 104

XII. The Last Great Scene, Tell It All 112

XIII. The Last of the South 121

LIFE AND SERVICE SERIES

EVIDENCES are not wanting of an increasing popular demand for short courses in Bible study and courses dealing with various practical aspects and problems of the Christian life in its larger relationships. Such studies are demanded for use as elective courses in adult Bible classes, among voluntary study groups in colleges and preparatory schools and for High School credit in weekday religious instruction.

In order to meet these various needs it is proposed to provide as rapidly as may be consistent with a high standard of excellence, a variety of short courses to be known as the Life and Service Series. There will be included in this series studies in selected important portions of the Old and New Testaments, together with courses in practical ethics, social service, Christian doctrine and other subjects of special interest to the groups for which these studies are intended.

The treatment of the subject matter in each case, while popular in style, will be scholarly in spirit and modern in point of view, suitable alike for class work and for individual study.

It is desirable that each member of the class studying the parables have a copy of the Studies and as far as possible read and reflect upon the chapter before the session. He will then, like the householder "who bringeth forth out of his treasure things new and old," be ready to contribute helpfully to the discussion in class and to profit the more by its fruits.

A simple and rewarding order of study is this: First read Professor Moffatt's translation of the parable at the beginning of the lesson, comparing it with other versions. When the Gospels give parallel accounts of the parables these should be read. They are as follows: Chapter I, Matthew 18. 10-14; III, Mark 4. 1-20, Luke 8. 4-8; IV, Luke 6. 46-49; IX, Luke 19. 11-27; XII, Mark 4. 30-32, Luke 13. 18-21. Endeavor to see with the mind's eye the incident recorded by the parable in all its vividness. Then read the chapter thoughtfully. It will be noticed that here and there in the text occur unanswered questions. The wise reader will stop to reflect upon them for his own sake. Similar questions will be found at the end of each chapter. In the class session these and others may be discussed. In all the chapters the light which the parable throws on the character of Jesus and on the nature of his Kingdom should be considered. And, finally, "be ye doers of the Word and not hearers only."

THE EDITORS.

A WORD FROM THE AUTHOR

"THE parts of the Bible that I like best," said an old Scotch lady to Dr. Thomas Guthrie, "are the likes." She unconsciously spoke for a large section of the world. "The kingdom of heaven is like"—these are among the most enchanted words of human speech. For nineteen centuries the world has listened with eager heart to the great Teacher unfolding the truths of God and life in the matchless stories of the parables. Age cannot wither nor custom stale the infinite variety of their application to human life, its problems and its needs.

The present studies do not attempt to present a fresh exposition of the parables dealt with. No part of the Bible has been more adequately treated. The chapters aim, rather, to make an application of the parables to the conditions of present-day life in a manner that may be suggestive and helpful for Bible class study and discussion. One sure effect of such a study in the light of the complex conditions of modern life is that we are struck with a new amazement at the limitless range of their application to all sorts and conditions of life and the timelessness of their message. We realize with a fresh sense of their truth the words of Jesus: "Heaven and earth shall pass away, but my words shall not pass away."

In the text of the chapters the quotations from the Bible are from the American Revised Version. For the sake, however, of the freshness and insight which the reading of a new translation gives, each chapter has been prefaced by the parable as it occurs in the recent translation of the New Testament by Professor James Moffatt, the noted English scholar. It is believed that students and readers of the Word will welcome the opportunity to read and compare this with the older and more familiar versions.

HALFORD E. LUCCOCK.

BIBLIOGRAPHY

For the student of the parables there is a rich and easily accessible literature. The titles of a few of the best-known and most useful books of exposition are given below. Grateful acknowledgment for constant help is freely made to these and to other writers and commentators on the Gospels.

Marcus Dods. The Parables of Our Lord. Methodist Book Concern. One volume is on the parables in Matthew and one on those in Luke. These are probably the best for the teacher and the general student.

Richard C. Trench. Notes on the Parables. Fleming H. Revell Co.

A. B. Bruce. The Parabolic Teaching of Christ. Methodist Book Concern.

G. H. Hubbard. The Teaching of Jesus in Parables. The Pilgrim Press. This is the most recent exposition of the parables and very suggestive.

Various English Authors. The Parables of Jesus. Methodist Book Concern.

CHAPTER I

THE LOST SHEEP.   THE LOST COIN

Luke 15. 1-10

Now the taxgatherers and sinners were all approaching him to listen to him, but the Pharisees and the scribes complained, "He welcomes sinners and eats along with them!" So he told them this parable, "Which of you with a hundred sheep, if he loses one, does not leave the ninety-nine in the desert and go after the lost one till he finds it? When he finds it he puts it on his shoulders with joy, and when he gets home he gathers his friends and neighbours: 'Rejoice with me,' he says to them, 'for I have found the sheep I lost.' So, I tell you, there will be joy in heaven over a single sinner who repents, more than over ninety-nine good people who do not need to repent. Or again, suppose a woman has ten shillings. If she loses one of them, does she not light a lamp and scour the house and search carefully till she finds it? And when she finds it she gathers her women-friends and neighbours, saying, 'Rejoice with me, for I have found the shilling I lost.' So, I tell you, there is joy in the presence of the angels of God over a single sinner who repents."

How These Parables Touch Us

Some one has called Jesus Christ "the great contemporary." To each new century and to each new generation he speaks with an unfailing timeliness. The central ideas of the three parables of the lost, the Lost Sheep, the Lost Coin, and the Prodigal Son, touch very closely some dominating interests of present day life and thought. They deal with "the lost," with God's treatment of them and our treatment. They represent an interest so compelling in the life of Jesus that they are frequently called "the Gospel in the Gospel." It is an interest which is closely related to the vast and increasing concern of modern life in lost things and their reclamation and conservation.

We see this interest on every hand. Widespread attention to loss of life is shown in the "safety first" movement in railroading and industry. It appears in the conquest of preventable diseases, such as tuberculosis, typhoid, and the elimination of preventable blindness. We see also a nation-wide interest in lost resources, an awakening to the waste of natural wealth and power. More recently we have developed a new interest in lost energy and the saving of energy and motion made possible by scientific management. During the last fifteen years three words have had a great vogue in our national thought and speech, each representing a great interest in wasted powers—uplift, conservation, and efficiency. Again there was never a time when men were asking more earnestly what should be the attitude of society to its outcasts, the delinquent, the criminal, and convict. Are prisons for punishment or reform? What shall be our personal attitude to offenders? These are "live" questions to-day. Thus nothing could be more contemporaneous with present interests than the words of Jesus, "The Son of man came to seek and to save that which was lost." These were the controlling interests of Jesus—the uplift of men, the conservation of spiritual resources and the efficient direction of life.

THE HISTORY OF A SNEER

These parables were called forth by the murmuring sneer of the Pharisees and scribes, when the publicans and outcasts drew near to hear Jesus—"This man receiveth sinners and eateth with them." "Who can refute a sneer?" asks Paley. Time has refuted this sneer of the Pharisees, for it is now chiefly interesting for the unimpeachable testimony it gives of the attraction which Jesus had for "sinners," those who were regarded as outcasts in strict religious circles. The very words have become the highest tribute ever paid to Jesus, "the Friend of sinners." Very frequently sinful men avoid a man of spotless character and reputation. Why was it different in Jesus' case? Why is it that so much that is commonly termed goodness today repels rather than attracts men? How can this result be avoided?

COMMON ELEMENTS IN THREE PARABLES

There are two great teachings set forth with transparent clearness and cumulative force in the three parables of the Lost Sheep, the Lost Coin, and the Prodigal Son. They are the very essence of the teaching of Jesus: God's estimate of man's value; and the contrast between the active, seeking love of God and the Pharisaic attitude of loveless indifference to the lost.

GOD'S ESTIMATE OF MAN'S VALUE

The picture which Jesus so tenderly draws of the shepherd leaving the ninety-nine sheep, to go and search for the one which had wandered away, sets forth irresistibly the value which one man has for God. The Fatherhood of God means that nothing else can ever take the place of a son in the Father's heart.

As civilization increases in complexity and the bounds of knowledge expand, there is more and more need for the revelation which Jesus brought of a God in whose eyes every man has an eternal place which is for himself alone. Many forces to-day impel men to feel the littleness and insignificance of the individual. The vast universe disclosed by science has given to many people an almost crushing sense of the small importance of an individual human life. If the psalmist, as he looked up into the heavens, was overawed by the thought, "What is man, that thou art mindful of him?" how much more overwhelming is our sense of the immensity of the universe! Where the psalmist saw only a few thousand stars we may look through a Lick telescope and see millions. One effect of the theory of evolution has been to give to many people an idea of nature in which the individual counts for little more than the bubble on the crest of the wave.

> "So careful of the type she seems,
> So careless of the single life."

The factory system, where a man seems like a small cog interlocked with thousands of others in a vast impersonal machine, and where the men are usually designated by a

number, distinctly lessens the value placed on each man.
Low wages are another cause of the diminishing estimate
of a man's worth. To the question once asked by Jesus,
"How much is a man better than a sheep?" the sad answer may be returned from a thousand factory towns and
mines, "No better!" There is still point to the bitter cry
of Thomas Hood uttered fifty years ago:

> "O God! that bread should be so dear
> And flesh and blood so cheap!"

The influence of nationalism, particularly in war, when
men are simply units in a great national force, with its
emphasis on the aggregate mass rather than the personal
units which compose it, has had the same general effect.

The picture of man's value given by Jesus in this parable
supplies a wholesome corrective to this tendency. We
have had quite enough "bird's-eye views" of men, in which
they seem very small and insignificant. We need a view
of man as he appears in God's eyes, with a unique value
which all the rest of creation cannot replace. When a
child wanders away from him, God has the heartache and
sense of loss which an earthly parent feels. Do we usually
think of sin in its effect on the one who sins rather than
on God who grieves for his child? Which aspect is principally in view in this parable? Is this conception of God as
actively interested in the welfare of every man commonly
held? What is the usual conception of God held by the
average man who is not actively religious?

THE BASIS OF DEMOCRACY

The picture of the impartial love and concern of God
for the last, the least, and the lost, is the most thoroughgoing basis for democracy ever set forth. How it strikes
at the root of every kind of special privilege! of national
pride! Small wonder that the Pharisees saw their own
structure of exclusiveness tottering to its fall under Jesus'
teaching! The parable virtually creates all men equal in
the sight of God. The Pharisees were spiritual "snobs."
What bearing has this parable on present-day snobbery?
James Russell Lowell said that there was "dynamite enough

in the New Testament to blow civilization to pieces." This parable is full of social dynamite in the sense that it "blows to pieces" many pretensions to exclusive worth. Why is it that social and religious inequality and exclusiveness of class and caste have been sanctioned for so long by people who profess Christianity? What kinds of snobbery exist in the world to-day?

WHEN IS A MAN "LOST"?

Is your usual conception of the term "lost" as used in the gospel that of a finally determined condition of a person, an eternal destiny? Do you think it has that meaning in this parable? Does not the word "lost" seem, rather, to mean that "the soul is in the grip of forces which, if left to themselves, will sooner or later bring disaster"? (McConnell.) The sheep had not come to destruction when the shepherd found it. It was lost simply because it was wandering in the wilderness without a leader. Jesus seems to have in mind, then, people who have lost their direction in life. Like the sheep in the wilderness, they are living wandering, aimless, drifting lives. A man is lost, in Jesus' conception, when he has lost his direction, when his life is a succession of thoughts and actions which are not directed to the true end of life or controlled by a right purpose. He may or may not be immoral or dissipated. His "lostness" is not determined by whether or not he indulges in the gratification of appetite, but by whether his life has true direction and worthy purpose. How does faith in Christ restore a man who is lost in the sense in which we have been discussing the term? What light does this parable throw on what it means to be "saved"?

SUBSTITUTES FOR THE SEARCH OF THE SHEPHERD

This parable has an outlook in two directions. In it Jesus reveals the character of God. He also gives a model for human action. The point of these stories was in the phrase, "Go thou and do likewise." What stirred the Pharisees to wrath was Jesus' insistence that any other attitude toward sinful men than that of positive, seeking love was unlike God's attitude and hence wrong. The attitude of the Pharisees could not stand the strong light of comparison with God's attitude. How well does your habitual attitude toward those who have wandered away in evildoing stand the same comparison? Is it one of earnest good will which refuses to be stopped from active efforts toward restoration? Is any other attitude really Christian?

Consider some ways of thinking about those who have wandered. Have you ever heard these excuses made by Christian people to explain why they were not more concerned with others' welfare? Have you ever thought in a similar way yourself?

"They will probably come back all right." Did you ever know of any Sunday school scholars lost permanently to the church because their teacher had this lazy idea of duty?

"The great majority are safe."

"It's their own fault."

"It is not my business to go after them." What light does this parable throw on what *is* a Christian's business?

"They are not worth much anyhow." This may seem to be so heartless as to be very uncommon, but is it? Have you ever heard any opinions about the natives of non-Christian countries which sounded like this?

THE LOST COIN: GOD SEEKING A LOST FORCE

In addition to the common elements which it shares with the parable of the Lost Sheep, the Lost Coin adds the idea that we are not only necessary to God's love but also to his purposes. A coin is so much compressed power. It has purchasing value, and its loss to the woman represented just that much less ability to bring about her purposes and desires. God is a Father desiring to restore his family circle; but he is also the Builder of a kingdom, and for a son to be away from him means the loss of so much potential energy for bringing in that order of society which we call his Kingdom. Jesus continually thought of men in terms of their possibilities. It was so when he looked on Peter and said to him, "Thou art Simon"; "thou shalt be called Peter." As Jesus looked on men who had wandered away into sin he beheld a great loss of spiritual energy. As we look on men do we usually think of what they might be and do to help to establish the kingdom of God? Think of the relation of your own abilities to the tasks of the Kingdom in your community. Is all your possible force at the disposal of God?

The coin was not lost in the sense that its value was destroyed. "It was just as good as it ever was. It was lost simply in that it was out of right relations. It had been swept out with the dust or had rolled off into the corner or down through the crack. If we may carry out the suggestiveness of the word itself, it was lost because it was out of circulation" (McConnell). We see from this more clearly how large a meaning the word "lost" had for Jesus as he applied it to men. This idea of a man's being lost when he is out of helpful contact with his fellow men is the same truth as that expressed elsewhere by Jesus: "He that saveth his life shall lose it." Whoever holds himself aloof from sympathetic and sacrificial contact with men is a long distance away from the purpose which God has for him, no matter how rigidly he has observed legal requirements. Righteousness, in Jesus' mind, always included social helpfulness, the continual giving of one's life in daily circulation among others. He came to seek and to save those lost in this manner, that they might be restored to a right working relationship to God and so become an available part of God's force in the world.

How do men to-day become lost and separated from helpful contact with others? Many men are lost behind the cash register. Instead of finding any outlet for their energies in broad human sympathies and service, their sole passion is for making entries under "Cash Received." They well deserve Goldsmith's famous epitaph on Burke,

> "Who, born for the universe, narrowed his mind,
> And to party gave up what was meant for mankind."

For such a one George Sand suggested the epitaph—"Born a man, died a grocer." Others allow some specialty to remove them almost entirely from the world's need. "They are like a needle, just as sharp and just as narrow." Others are lost in their homes. They find a selfish content within

their own pleasant four walls and close their eyes to outside need. As far as helping forward the kingdom of
God is concerned, a man may be as useless in a busy office
or a quiet library as in a saloon. What are the strongest
motives which may be brought to bear on an isolated selfish
life?

TURNING THE WORLD UPSIDE DOWN

The picture of the woman diligently sweeping the whole
house to find the lost coin presents the truth that seeking
the lost is a very upsetting business. While it was going
on, the woman's house was literally turned upside down,
making it very uncomfortable for everyone in the house.
The enterprise of winning men back to God is a very upsetting process in the world to-day. It involves disturbance
of comfort and long established use and custom. It involves another thing, and that the sorest point of all—
profits. The social conditions under which men live must
frequently be changed before the lost can really be reached
by the message or effective evangelistic work done. The
profits of many a business founded on special privilege,
the payment of wages below a living standard, the traffic
in things which debase and debauch men—these things
must be changed as a necessary part of seeking the lost.
Hence many people prefer to be left undisturbed in their
ease under the old conditions rather than establish new
conditions under which the lost may be reclaimed. Take,
for instance, a mill town where men are worked long hours
for low wages and charged excessive prices at a company
store, where child labor abounds and saloons flourish.
What does seeking the lost mean there? It calls for exactly what the woman who lost the coin did in her house—
the changing of things about so that the people may be
really reached. Why do some business men insist that the
minister should preach the "simple gospel" whenever he
begins to attack some strongly established evil? What do
they mean by the "simple gospel"? What is the "simple
gospel"?

FOR REFLECTION AND DISCUSSION

The parables are often called the "World's Greatest Short

Stories." How would you compare Jesus with others of the world's great story-tellers? With Æsop or Bunyan, for example?

What forces in modern life have had the effect of lessening the value and importance of the individual man? How does the teaching of Jesus counteract these forces?

Is the work of winning men back to God harder to-day than it was fifty years ago? Give reasons for your answer.

Is there greater temptation to-day for men to wander away from religious influences than a century ago? In what respects?

What bearing have these parables on the subject of the treatment of the criminal?

Is "snobbery" a sin? What is a snob? With how many different kinds of snobs are you familiar?

What modern parallels to the attitude of the Pharisees toward the publicans and outcasts can you think of?

Why do some people find it hard to believe in God's deep concern for the salvation and welfare of one man?

How may a real concern for the restoration of men to their best possibilities be cultivated?

CHAPTER II

THE PRODIGAL SON

Luke 15. 11-32

He also said: "There was a man who had two sons, and the younger said to his father, 'Father, give me the share of the property that falls to me.' So he divided his means among them. Not many days later, the younger son sold off everything and went abroad to a distant land, where he squandered his means in loose living. After he had spent his all, a severe famine set in throughout that land, and he began to feel in want; so he went and attached himself to a citizen of that land, who sent him to his fields to feed swine. And he was fain to fill his belly with the pods the swine were eating; no one gave him anything. But when he came to his senses he said, 'How many hired men of my father have more than enough to eat, and here am I perishing of hunger! I will be up and off to my father, and I will say to him, "Father, I have sinned against heaven and before you; I don't deserve to be called your son any more; only make me like one of your hired men."' So he got up and went off to his father. But when he was still far away his father saw him and felt pity for him and ran to fall upon his neck and kiss him. The son said to him, 'Father, I have sinned against heaven and before you; I don't deserve to be called your son any more.' But the father said to his servants, 'Quick, bring the best robe and put it on him, give him a ring for his hand and sandals for his feet, and bring the fatted calf, kill it, and let us eat and be merry; for my son here was dead and he has come to life, he was lost and he is found.' So they began to make merry. Now his elder son was out in the field, and as he came near the house he heard music and dancing; so, summoning one of the servants, he asked what this meant. The servant told him, 'Your brother has arrived, and your father has killed the fatted calf because he has got him back safe and sound.' This angered him, and he would not go in. His father came out and tried to appease him, but he replied, 'Look at all the years I have been serving you! I have never neglected any of your orders, and yet you have never given me so much as a kid, to let me make merry with my friends. But as soon as this son of yours arrives, after having wasted your means with harlots, you kill the fatted calf for him!' The father

18

said to him, 'My son, you and I are always together, all I have is yours. We could not but make merry and rejoice, for your brother here was dead and has come to life again, he was lost but he has been found.'"

THE TWO LOST SONS

ALL generations of Christians have agreed in calling the story of the Prodigal Son the Pearl of Parables. Judged either by its literary form or by the importance of its spiritual truth, it holds an unrivaled place, not only in the Bible, but in the world's literature. The story of the prodigal's journeying and return is told with such matchless beauty and simplicity and contains such an infinitely tender appeal to all wanderers, and such an assurance of welcome from the father, that it is enshrined in the world's affections.

This must not obscure from us the point that, as Jesus told the parable, it was a story of two lost sons. His attention was not given solely to the prodigal. It was to the portrait of the elder brother that Jesus chiefly invited the attention of the Pharisees who complained of his association with sinners. He drew their own portrait in the elder brother and let them "see themselves as others see them," above all, as God sees them in their loveless contempt and indifference to the lost. Jesus showed that the son who stayed at home was just as much lost, because he was as far away from his father in spirit, as the boy who wandered away. Keep this in mind during your study. Have you been accustomed to think of a certain class of people and a certain class of acts when you hear the word "sinners"? What kind of acts were they? What light does this parable throw on your idea of what a "sinner" is?

"BREAKING HOME TIES"

The prodigal's story portrays in telling strokes the natural history of lawlessness. The self-willed desire of the prodigal to "see life," to lay out life for himself and for his own pleasure, lay at the bottom of the prodigal's

sin and lies at the bottom of all moral evil. The rest of
the story, with its record of gross sin, is just the natural
unfolding of that attitude. While the prodigal was still
at home, chafing under the restraint of his father's house,
wishing he were away from the home, he already made
the beginning of his sin and tragedy. "A darkened heart
is the far country," says Saint Augustine, "for it is not
by our feet but by our affections that we either leave Thee
or return unto Thee."

The prodigal gives very different names to his actions
at the end. When his father divided unto him the inheritance, no doubt he proudly referred to his situation as
"independence." He was a man now, no longer tied to anyone. He would show people what a bright young man
with money and no hampering limitations could do. While
the life in the far country was at the height of its excite-
ment he would call it, with much gusto, "seeing life."
Later, when his funds were gone, and, with them, his
fair-weather friends, it was a case of "hard luck." Only
as he went through the last full measure of painful want
and was making his way back to his father, did he find
the real name for all these high-sounding illusions.
"Father, I have sinned," he cried, seeing the truth squarely
at last. It had been sin under all these masquerades.
This inability to give the right names to our actions is a
constant accompaniment of sin. There is no surer moral
safeguard, as well as no higher moral duty, than that of
calling things by their right names. Do you see clearly
in this regard? Do you ever call by an agreeable name
an action of yours which in reality is much less agreeable?

The Tragedy of the Far Country

There was a twofold tragedy for the prodigal in the far
country—waste and its inevitable sequel, want. The
picture of the rioting career of the prodigal is one familiar
to all ages, and a more pitiable spectacle earth never sees—
the waste of power, of possibilities, of dreams and ideals
and hopes of youth. All these priceless jewels of personality are carelessly thrown into the mire of sensuality.

While this tragedy of waste caused by sensual appetites

is a common one, it is by no means the only one. The far country of bodily appetites is not the only one to which men travel to wreck their lives of their best possibilities. The journey need not end in a literal pigpen. "Every waster is a prodigal," and whoever wastes in any irresponsible manner the powers and time which God has given him is a prodigal. It is significant that in the novel by Winston Churchill called The Far Country the sin into which the hero of the story is led is not the dissipation of appetite so much as the loss of his early inherited ideals and the gradual lowering of his standards of right and wrong in the practice of his profession. What kinds of waste do you think of other than that of the appetites?

It is an accurate picture of life which Jesus draws when he relates that after the waste of riotous living, "there arose a mighty famine in that country, and he began to be in want." Want always follows waste. The friends who helped him spend his money scatter rapidly when it is all gone and he faces the famine alone. In utter destitution he is reduced to the worst ignominy which could be thrust upon a Jew. The enforced labor in the pig sty speaks eloquently of the enslaving character of sin. This is the end of his boisterous quest for liberty—a compelled swineherd! It is the end of every search for liberty by way of license. "Every man who sets out for what he calls liberty, using the world as a servant to minister to his pleasures, must submit to having the relations reversed so that the world uses him as its drudge and sin as its slave." The man who takes alcoholic liquor as a means of finding "liberty" from the cares and anxieties of daily life illustrates this enslaving character of appetite. It does give a temporary freedom from the weight of the responsibilities of life, but all the time it fastens a new bondage upon the man's life.

The hunger of the ragged boy in the pig sty, so famished that he would eat the husks that the swine ate, well pictures the bankruptcy to which vicious dissipation brings a man. It brings financial dissipation, as it came to the prodigal. This is the least part of the bankruptcy of sin. But even here, when we think of money as compressed power and think of the vast possibilities for good it contains, the squandering of money in gratification of a base appetite is a tragic waste. But far worse than financial loss is the physical damage which it brings, the effects of which are permanent and which extend their curse frequently through the next generation, and even beyond that. We never reckon the full effects of a young man's "having his fling" at sin and "sowing his wild oats" without considering the children born to heritages of sickness, blindness, or feeble-mindedness through the sins of the fathers.

"When a Man Comes to Himself"

In this extremity of misfortune the homesick, famishing boy remembers the plenty of his father's house. The illusions of sin are gone and in their place he sees clearly the ugly realities of the consequences of dissipation. As these realities were seen, "he came to himself." What do you think these words of Jesus imply about the nature of sin? Does it seem to indicate that in Jesus' mind the vicious impulses were not the real man, and that when he was dominated by them he was not himself? Note how deeply this expression of Jesus has affected our use of language. When a man does a thing poorly, how quick we are to excuse him and say, "He's not himself to-day!" In which way do we arrive at the fairest estimate of a man —when we judge his worst side and worst mood to be the real man, or his best? Which method of judgment prevails more among the people you know?

There are several levels in "coming to oneself." It is a lifelong process really to "come to oneself" and find the true reach of one's capacities and the utmost possibilities of one's service. For the prodigal in the barnyard it was leaving the far country of sin that was the result of coming to himself. But there were other and later steps to be taken after he got home in order to reach the full possibilities of his personality in service. Is there not some step for you right now—some higher ideal of personal life, some additional service undertaken, some habit relinquished, which shall be a coming to yourself in a larger way for you?

GOD'S ANSWER TO REPENTANCE

While he is yet a great way off the father's eager eyes discern the returning boy and he runs out to meet him. He erects no barriers of reproach. He does not scrutinize his son's motives for coming back. His heart is filled only with a flood of joy that the long lost boy has returned and the welcome is unconditional and complete. God is quick to discern the faintest movement of the heart toward him. "He takes ten steps to our one."

The prodigal's honest confession is well worth noting. He makes no effort to excuse himself. He does not try to soften matters and speak of his "faults" and "failings." He does not say, "I have been a little wild." He does not try to put the blame on his companions or lug in that scapegoat on which the blame of a million sins is placed —"circumstances." Could the father have treated him in the same forgiving way if he had tried to defend or excuse his action? Do you ever find Jesus making allowances for a man who makes allowances for himself? What excuses do you find most often given for sin to-day?

THE JOY OF RELIGION

The fifteenth chapter of Luke tells the story of three merrymakings. Joy over the restored runs through all these stories. In Jesus' estimate, joy was an ever-present element of religion. Why is it that the religion of so many people frequently lacks a deep feeling of joy and becomes such a staid, colorless business? Is not one part of the reason that there is so little real longing for others in it? It was because the shepherd had cared so much and searched so earnestly that he felt such unrestrained joy over the finding. It was because the father loved the prodigal that he sent for the best robe and the ring. The joy we get out of our religion depends on the earnestness which we put into it.

PRESERVATION VS. RESCUE

Beautiful as the story of the prodigal's return is, with its tender pictures of forgiveness and penitence and restoration, one cannot help thinking how much finer it would have been if he had never gone away into the far country of sin at all. How much more beautiful, happy, and useful his life would have been, if, instead of the wasted physical vigor, never wholly regained, the bitter memories, the wasted time, never to be recovered, the impaired capacities and lessened influence, he had grown up at home into a fully developed manhood with all its powers preserved and disciplined! How much more of worth would unbroken companionship with his father have put into his life! As we hold these two possible life courses together in our minds does it not suggest forcibly how much greater a thing the preservation of a boy from a life of sin is than rescuing him after he has gone the full length? Which of these two forms of work yields the larger results? What measures may be utilized in keeping a boy from wandering away into gross sin? Do the boys of your church find in it a legitimate outlet for their energies and enthusiasm and spirits so that they do not need to find it outside in questionable and dangerous places? How about the boys of your community? What is your class doing to safeguard the boys of your neighborhood or town?

THE ELDER BROTHER

No comment on the elder brother could make the contrast between the father's welcome and the elder brother's spirit so glaring as the simple reading of the parable. To turn from the father to the elder brother is like stepping from the flower-laden air of June into a nipping December chill. In the father there is the throbbing overflow of joy; in the elder brother every genial current of the soul is frozen. In the father's whole action and speech we feel the self-forgetfulness of a generous emotion. The only emotion which touches the elder brother is the venomous one of sullen, self-centered jealousy. The salvation of his brother from destruction; his restoration to honor and love, the healing of the breach in the home—all these, which should have stirred the blood of a brother's heart, left no impression upon his. In every word he speaks the hard rasp of selfishness is heard. In the first sentence he speaks he refers to himself five times! He will not call his brother by that name, but in what seems the most cruel touch of all, he speaks of him to his father as "Thy son."

Though all this time he had been busy about the affairs of his father, he did not share at all his father's love for the other boy. He did not even love his father, or he would have rejoiced at the great happiness which had come to him. He had stayed at home and worked all these years, not because by doing so he could be with the father he loved and help him, for that plainly meant nothing to him. He had stayed in the spirit of mechanical, slavish drudgery, doubtless because he had figured out that it would pay. It is possible for persons to be actively engaged in church work and yet have little or no religious interest and little concern for those outside. What effect does this have on the church? How can such a condition be prevented?

The elder brother was also quite wrong in his idea of righteousness. He showed this when he said to his father, "I never transgressed a commandment." It was all negative. The Pharisees rated themselves righteous on account of the number of things they abstained from doing. Jesus' idea of goodness was never merely the absence of bad things. It always included positive, good actions. What effect does it have on a man's character when his idea of goodness and righteousness is negative? Give examples of your answer. A very materialistic thought of reward was also the elder brother's. He thought only of things. Saint Augustine made the pertinent comment centuries ago that the elder brother looked to the getting of something from God, in preference to possessing all things in God. To a true son the father's love and companionship are a reward beyond all else. It is Jesus' teaching that the highest reward of a child of God is the Father himself and not any gifts or benefits. Can a person be really a Christian who is so because it pays?

The elder brother warns each of us of the danger of the "sins of the disposition." With all his vigor and earnestness Jesus pointed out the enormity of unbrotherliness, contempt, and pride. The most scathing denunciations he ever pronounced were launched against those sins as they appeared in the Pharisees. The elder brother embodies these sins, and they are just as ugly and destructive to the finer qualities of the spirit as the coarser dissipation of the younger brother. Is it as easy to recognize these sins of the disposition, such as jealousy, selfishness, avarice, unbrotherliness, pride, contempt, as sins of appetite? How may one guard against them?

If the Prodigal Had Met His Brother First

Suppose the prodigal had met his elder brother before he had met his father, what would have happened? He would have gone back to the far country undoubtedly. He would have been discouraged from his purpose to come back by the cold, suspicious, cynical attitude of his brother. What a terrible ending it would have made to the story!

Bring this possibility close home. What do you think does happen in thousands of similar cases? Are not many wanderers kept away from their father's house because they meet the elder brother in the vestibule? Are you the elder brother whom some returning sinner has met? It is a very serious thing to consider that the only chance some people have of seeing the Father God is what they see of him in our character and action. Is your attitude to those trying to lift themselves out of a bad past into a better future anything like that of the prodigal's father?

For Reflection and Discussion

What is the difference between willfulness and self-reliance?

What contrast do you find between the request of the prodigal, "Give me my portion of the inheritance," and the spirit of the petition in the Lord's Prayer, "Give us this day our daily bread"?

Why does distance from home mean a moral testing? What is a man's real character, what he is at home or what he is when away?

As opposed to the quickly exhausted pleasures of dissipation, what would you name as "the durable satisfactions of life"?

Which is the easier way to judge men, at their best or at their worst?

Do you think the "sins of disposition are harder to over-come than the sins of appetite"? Why do you think as you do?

When the prodigal was wasting his substance, did he enjoy freedom? What is freedom? Is it freedom to do what we please in defiance of all the laws that surround us?

CHAPTER III

THE PARABLE OF THE SOWER

Matthew 13. 1-9, 18-25

That same day Jesus went out of the house and seated himself by the seaside; but, as great crowds gathered to him, he entered a boat and sat down, while all the crowd stood on the beach. He spoke at some length to them in parables, saying: "A sower went out to sow, and as he sowed some seeds fell on the road and the birds came and ate them up. Some other seeds fell on stony soil where they had not much earth, and shot up at once because they had no depth of soil; but when the sun rose they got scorched and withered away because they had no root. Some other seeds fell among thorns, and the thorns sprang up and choked them. Some other seeds fell on good soil and bore a crop, some a hundredfold, some sixty, and some thirtyfold. He who has an ear, let him listen to this." . . .

Now, listen to the parable of the sower. When anyone hears the word of the Realm and does not understand it, the evil one comes and snatches away what has been sown in his heart; that is the man who is sown 'on the road.' As for him who is sown 'on stony soil,' that is the man who hears the word and accepts it at once with enthusiasm; he has no root in himself, he does not last, but when the word brings trouble or persecution he is at once repelled. As for him who is sown 'among thorns,' that is the man who listens to the word, but the worry of the world and the delight of being rich choke the word; so it proves unfruitful. As for him who is sown 'on good soil,' that is the man who hears the word and understands it; he bears fruit, producing now a hundredfold, now sixty, and now thirtyfold."

A PARABLE OF HEARING

IT is no accident that the Parable of the Sower is placed first of all the parables. It has this place because it deals with a matter which is preliminary to all real effectiveness

28

of the gospel, the matter of hearing. This parable is not a sermon on what the truth of the kingdom of God is, so much as it is a sermon on how to hear the truth. Before Jesus tells his followers the truth of the Kingdom in other parables he warns them earnestly in this one, "Take heed how ye hear." This becomes more clear if we think of it as "The Parable of the Soils," rather than by the name which it has received from its opening words, the Parable of the Sower. The sower and the seed, so far as the story goes, do not receive the main emphasis. The object of emphasis and importance is the soil and the influence which different kinds of soil have on the harvest. Its one great truth is that just as the harvest depends on the kind of soil into which the seed falls, so the effect and power of God's truth in the world depend on the condition of heart and mind of those who hear it. The whole parable is a forcible commentary on the words of Proverbs—"Keep thy heart with all diligence; for out of it are the issues of life."

A BIT OF JESUS' AUTOBIOGRAPHY

"All great literature," says Robertson Nicoll, "is autobiography." By this he means that the writing which has made the deepest impression on the world has expressed a real experience or first-hand observation of the author. The story of the sower illustrates this, for it undoubtedly expresses the experience of Jesus himself. What has been true of the reception of the gospel by different types of hearers through all the history of Christianity was first true in the experience of its Founder. The parable carries conviction as a description of life because it came out of life. Jesus himself was "a sower who went forth to sow." It may well have been that even as he looked out over his audience by the lakeside he saw before him all these kinds of hearers. Many of the Pharisees were "wayside hearers" with minds so hardened that his new truth could not enter. He had met again and again the impulsive followers without depth, whose allegiance was not proof against hardship or toil. Too well he knew the disciple whose good purposes were crowded out by other interests, like the one who an-

swered Jesus' call to discipleship by pleading to be allowed
to wait until his father died (Luke 9. 59) ; or the one who
wished to postpone his discipleship for social duties (Luke
9. 61).   Of this class Jesus sadly said, "No man, having
put his hand to the plow, and looking back, is fit for the
kingdom of God."   Think of the life and teaching of Jesus
in connection with these different kinds of hearers.   Large
multitudes heard him; only a mere handful became his
permanent disciples.   What was the reason?   To which of
these three classes of hearers do you think that most of
those who fell away from Jesus belonged?

Four Kinds of Soil

The portrayal of these four different conditions of mind
and heart, which may describe one man at different times
and under different conditions or different men, falls into
four natural divisions: the hard life, the shallow life, the
crowded life, and the fruitful life.

The Hard Life

Jesus had noticed that some seed produced no fruit because it did not get into the ground.   It fell on a footpath
across the field, where the ground had been tramped solid
and smooth, or in a cart-wheel track where it found no
entrance.   It had no more chance to grow there than it
would have on a smooth piece of marble.   The soil, once
as good as any other soil, had been trampled on so constantly that it was hard and impervious.   The seed would
lie on the surface as on a pavement and the birds would
soon pick it up.

It is just as impossible for truth to get into some minds,
Jesus said. They simply do not take it in. The mind throws
off the truth as a slated roof throws off hail.   Jesus' ex-
planation of this condition,—"heareth the word . . . and
understandeth it not,"—covers a multitude of very familiar
habits.   No one detail can be singled out and pointed to
with the words, "That is what it means to be a wayside
hearer."   In general, it means the attitude which regards
the Word of God as a thing apart from actual life, which

is not allowed a controlling place in determining conduct. For instance, religion is for many a formal thing, which never really stirs life. Perhaps they belong to a church-going family and their attitude to church going is that of mild thoughtless submission. In these circumstances, the preaching of God's truth, which ought to plow deep into their hearts and turn over the hard crust of custom and indifference, does not touch their will at all. Do you know many such hearers of the Word? Have you ever been one of them?

The mind becomes impenetrable, too, by the hardening effect of habit and the wearing of the daily routine. These processes may cause us to lose the capacity for impressions, to become hardened even to good. How may a person prevent habit and routine from destroying the openness of his mind and heart and the freshness and reality of his religion? Our minds may be impervious because of preju-dice. Why did the Pharisees form a prejudice against Jesus? What are your prejudices? How can a person overcome a prejudice? One of the worst habits of hearing is the common one of applying it all to some one else. Do you ever catch yourself thinking, when some plain truth is being spoken, "That certainly hits Jones pretty hard," or "Mrs. Smith must surely squirm under this"? It is so much easier generously to pass over the application of a truth to some one else than bravely and honestly to apply it to ourselves that this selfish habit soon becomes fixed.

What makes the mind throw off truth so readily is hearing it without putting it into practice. If we listen again and again to truth without striving to practice it, our power to respond to it steadily diminishes. Ruskin says, "Every duty we omit obscures some truth we might have known." William James makes a practical comment when he says, "Never suffer yourself to have an emotion without expressing it afterward in some active way."

The greatest need of a vast number of churchgoers is not more spiritual food, but more spiritual exercise. When you hear a strong presentation of truth, do you customarily try to find a way of practicing it?

The Shallow Life

Each class of hearers described by Jesus is an advance on the one before. The first class did not receive the seed at all. The second, like the shallow soil, opens a little. These hearers are attracted by the truth, see something of its value, but they do not allow it to root deeply enough. And so, because they are shallow rooted, the growth is checked. The blazing sun soon proves how superficial it is, for, having no roots to nourish life, it withers as quickly as it grew.

Jesus describes here the large number of people who have their minds open to the truth, but keep their hearts closed. They welcome the truth with impulsive joy, but when it begins to cost something to be a follower of Christ, when it means foregoing some pleasure, doing some hard duty, facing ridicule, forfeiting worldly success, their devotion wanes. The truth which wins the approval of the mind does not sink into the heart and command the will. It is easy enough to enjoy eloquent sermons, to pay compliments to the Bible, and be a Christian in theory. To make a persistent daily fight for character; to make real in our lives the ideals we admire—that is another matter. And that is all that makes our profession of any value whatever. Without that daily effort our religion is a scorched, dried-up plant.

Notice that the heat which caused the shallow-rooted plant to wither would have caused a well-rooted plant to grow all the more strongly and vigorously. It is just as true in the moral and spiritual sphere as in the physical. The same kind of tribulations and persecutions which made the apostle Paul even more determined in his loyalty to Christ caused others to renounce their Christian profession. The same persecutions under Nero and Diocletian which made some Christians gladly give their lives as martyrs made others slip back into paganism. How can "tribulation" really strengthen a man's character?

A common manifestation of the shallow life is seen in the flagging enthusiasm of Christian people whose active service is all in the past. They used to be active workers;

they used to teach in Sunday school. But that is ancient history. However enthusiastic they once were, the tide has receded and the rest of their lives is bounded by the shallows and miseries of a chronic lack of energy. Some one has said that there are four kinds of Christian workers: the tired, the retired, the tiresome, and the tireless. The "tired" and "retired" workers are familiar examples of this second class of hearers. The "problem of the unemployed" in Christian service is one of the hardest in extending the Kingdom. Are you part of that problem? Are you carried or do you lift?

The Crowded Life

The soil in which the good seed was choked by thorns represents the preoccupied minds and hearts in which the truth never brings forth its full fruits. Too many things are growing in the soil; too many interests have a place in the heart. The fertility of the soil is diverted from the wheat seed and goes to form thorn bushes.

This describes a familiar condition of our modern life. Artemus Ward once said that he "tried to do too much and succeeded." A great many are doing the same thing. They have so much on their minds and hearts that the influences of God are crowded out. The rush and movement of present-day life, teeming with a multitude of interests and responsibilities, accompanied by an increasing diversity of pleasures and a wide variety of appeals to the sense and mind, form a soil where the growing religious life is strangled for lack of room. If our religious life is to grow at all, it must grow by our making room for it among these very things. Hence the timeliness of the warning of this parable, which clearly calls to each of us —"Keep room for God."

When Jesus specifies the kind of weeds that crowd out the truth, he mentions two things, cares and riches. The danger of the crowded life does not lie alone with the rich; nor even with the poor. People who have neither poverty nor wealth face the time-consuming cares which threaten to strangle the religious life just as truly. Which is the more dangerous to the religious life, poverty or wealth?

Notice that "thorns" stand for any kind of weeds which will choke out the desired crop. They may be good in themselves, but "corn is a weed if it grows in a wheat field" (Hubbard). "The good is often the enemy of the best." Think how so good a thing as devotion to business may crowd out human sympathy and fellowship.

Such a thing as healthy recreation on Sunday, for instance, good in itself, may crowd out worship and make a whole life immeasurably poorer and weaker. Do we not usually approach the whole vexed question of amusements from the wrong angle? Men ask whether this particular thing is allowable or consistent, whether this pleasure is permitted or that gain defensible. Is not the real question, after all, not whether the particular act is wicked, but whether it dulls the edge of our interest in higher things and causes the spiritual life to lose its zest and joy and warm fervor?

The Fruitful Life

When we study the soil in which the seed sprang up and bore abundant fruit, we learn how the evil conditions in the other three kinds of soil may be overcome and our own lives made fruitful. Jesus explains the secret of fruitful hearing in the words, "These are such as in an honest and good heart, having heard the word, hold it fast, and bring forth fruit with patience." Jesus here emphasizes three qualities as necessary to fruitfulness of hearing: sincerity, meditation, and patience.

Sincerity. "An honest heart" means a preparedness to receive the truth, free from prejudices. We must not listen to the gospel with minds already made up or refuse to listen when it brings some unflattering truth home to us. An honest heart means a willingness to follow the truth even when that involves changing our conduct. An open mind does not mean absence of conviction. Many people talk in a boasting way about having an open mind when all they have is an empty head. What is the difference between the two?

Meditation. "Such as . . ., having heard the word, hold it fast." The Kingdom to-day greatly needs men

who will think over the Word of God till it becomes a part
of them. Emerson says that the hardest task in the world
is to think. One might almost be tempted to say also that it
is the rarest thing in the world. "It is not the amount of
knowledge you have, but the use you put it to,—it is not the
number of good sayings you have heard and can repeat that
will profit you, but the place in your hearts you have given
them and the connection they have with the motives, principles, and ruling ideas of your life" (Dods). Meditation
must not be confused with a lazy, hazy kind of day-dream-
ing or reverie. That leads to weakening of the mind and
will. Meditation is the hard thinking by which truth is
tied up closely to practical life. Why is it becoming a
lost art? What forces in present day life are hostile to
it? What means may be employed to keep it?

Patience. This too is an active rather than a passive
virtue. It means perseverance in the face of discouragement. Its symbol is not folded hands, but rather the
clenched hands of the farmer on the handles of the plow.
He looks down the long furrows with courageous perseverance for his task, willing to work and wait, because
he has faith in the seed and soil.

THE UNEXPECTED YIELD OF GOOD SOIL

In the seed in good ground bringing forth thirty, sixty,
and a hundredfold, Jesus asserts the abundant returns of
the spiritual world. If we keep our hearts open and recep-
tive, the truth which comes into them will bring forth
unexpected fruit in personal growth and increasing strength
of character and influence. Into each life which is kept
teachable and hospitable to the truth Christ continually
comes that we may have life and have it more abundantly.
The rich fullness of Christian personality with its un-
exhausted capacity for joy and service is a growth, sure
and unfailing, if the life is only open to the seed of God's
Word. The parable holds out to each of us the blessed
encouragement that our lives may become that marvelous
garden of God described by Paul: "The fruit of the Spirit
is love, joy, peace, longsuffering, kindness, goodness, faithfulness, meekness, self-control."

FOR REFLECTION AND DISCUSSION

Some people become impervious to new truth because their minds have become set and hardened. This usually comes after middle age, but sometimes comes earlier. What habits may a man cultivate to help him keep an open mind to new ideas?

Are the impressions made by the sermon on Sunday dissipated before they have a chance to sink deep? What is the reason? What effect does the conversation which follows the church service frequently have? What is the importance of quiet and order in the Sunday school?

What effect does a critical attitude toward the sermon have on the amount of good we get out of it?

How would you answer the question whether it is wrong to play golf on Sunday?

In what respects were the Pharisees wayside hearers of Jesus? Why are riches called "deceitful"?

What are the present-day forms of tribulation and persecution most dangerous? Does a Christian in ordinary circumstances ever experience persecution in these days? How about some of the ridicule and reputation for being "queer" which will meet a Christian in many quarters? What have you found to be the hardest things about Christian discipleship? Has it ever really cost you anything to be a Christian, in business, in social life? How much?

One valuable means of cultivating the religious life is the custom of family worship. If it has been crowded out of your home, what is the reason? Where the members of a family leave home at different times, what can be done to keep the values which were gained from morning family worship?

Why does some good soil bring forth one hundredfold while others bring forth only thirtyfold? To what may these differences refer in the realm of character? What light does the Parable of the Talents throw on this?

CHAPTER IV

THE TWO FOUNDATIONS

Matthew 7. 24-27

"Now, everyone who listens to these words of mine and acts upon them will be like a sensible man who built his house on rock. The rain came down, the floods rose, the winds blew and beat upon that house, but it did not fall, for it was founded on rock. And everyone who listens to these words of mine and does not act upon them will be like a stupid man who built his house on sand. The rain came down, the floods rose, the winds blew and beat upon that house, and down it fell— with a mighty crash."

When Jesus finished his speech, the crowds were astounded at his teaching; for he taught them like an authority, not like their own scribes.

THE LAST NAIL

THE Parable of the Two Foundations is the concluding appeal of the most important sermon ever delivered. It is the last nail with which the truth is driven home to the minds and hearts of those who listened to the Sermon on the Mount. It is impossible to imagine speech which could be packed into three verses of greater force than this indelible picture of the two builders. It takes that little word "do" and hurls it at us till it stings—"and doeth them." The truth which Jesus spoke was to be completed in action; and, until a man works out the truth in life, be it even such incomparable and matchless truth as the Sermon on the Mount, it is utterly worthless to him. Unless the truth of "these words of mine," Jesus declares, finds constant expression in daily life, the man who hears it will be just as helpless when life's real tests come, as a house set on the sand is in the teeth of a hurricane. "Therefore"

—the conclusion is as clear as the noonday sunlight—"do them."

Jesus never left truth hanging in the air as something remote from life, an abstract principle to which mild assent should be given. He was a model preacher in that he never considered a sermon finished until it was expressed in life and action. Have you ever heard the expression a "finished sermon"? What light does this parable throw on what a "finished sermon" ought to be? It does not take a vast amount of experience or observation to convince us that the great emphasis which Jesus gave to this necessity for action was well justified. Charts of exercise never made an athlete. Books on food never gave nourishment. Nor did sermons on righteousness ever make a saint. Charts, books, and sermons are useful for their purpose just in so far as they inspire and direct actual deeds.

TALK NO SUBSTITUTE FOR DEEDS!

This message is always necessary and timely because fine words are continually deceitful. We are likely to hear and talk about fine actions so much that we unconsciously come to think in a vague way that we have done them. Mark Twain says that if a man tells a story often enough, he will come to believe it. It is due to the same mental process that a clerk at the information desk of a railroad station has the feeling that he has actually been in the different cities and places, about which he has been supplying information every day for years. In both cases talk comes to be an acceptable substitute for real deeds. It is easy to listen; it is hard to do. To hear Jesus' sayings does not involve getting out of the easy chair of lazy self-satisfaction; to do them requires straightening all our moral muscles for action.

In Jesus' judgment, there can be no substitute for "doing." The world awards its applause differently. Masters of literature win its coveted verdict "Well said!" To the philosopher is awarded the commendation—"Well thought!" But fine speech and fine thought are not in themselves sufficient to win the approval of Jesus. They must express themselves in fine living. The approving verdict of Jesus is reserved for those to whom he can say "Well done!" Which more accurately represents your attitude to the gospel, your thoughts or your acts? Why?

A HOUSE ON A ROCK

It should be kept in mind that the thing which is compared to a rock foundation for a house is the doing of the teachings of Christ, as opposed to the mere hearing of them. The contrast is not drawn between the man who makes Christ and his teachings the foundation of his life and the man who builds on something else. The contrast is between the hearer who hears and does and the one who merely hears. One house rests on the rock of acts performed; the other on the sand of things merely heard.

Do these pictures, drawn by Jesus, correspond to the facts of life as you know it? What makes the picture true? Simply the fact that a strong character is largely the result of right habits and that right habits are established by action upon right impulses and principles. The rain and floods and the winds which assail the house in the parable represent those testing experiences and emergencies which can only be met successfully by that inner strength which has been created by action. The fire gong rings in a public school. The lives of a thousand children are in danger. Will the fire gong be the announcement of a terrible tragedy? It all depends on the training which the children have had whether instinctive responses and habits which can be trusted to carry them through the crisis, have been built up within them by action.

In the same way, the question whether severe tests in the realm of character are to be met successfully is decided by the amount of will power which has been created by the habit of daily obedience. The following sentences from the famous chapter on "Habit" by William James in his Psychology, form one of the strongest commentaries on this parable ever made. Read them carefully, with this parable in mind. "No matter how full a reservoir of *maxims* one may possess, and no matter how good one's *sentiments* may be, if one has not taken advantage of every concrete opportunity to *act,* one's character may remain entirely unaffected for the better. With mere good intentions hell is proverbially paved. And this is an obvious consequence of the principles we have laid down. A 'character,' as J. S. Mill says, 'is a completely fashioned will'; and a will, in the sense in which he means it, is an aggregate of tendencies to act in a firm and prompt and definite way upon all the principal emergencies of life. A tendency to act only becomes effectively ingrained in us in proportion to the uninterrupted frequency with which the actions actually occur, and the brain 'grows' to their use. When a resolve or a fine glow of feeling is allowed to evaporate without bearing practical fruit it is worse than a chance lost; it works so as positively to hinder future resolutions and emotions."[1]

Mobilizing the Will in Emergencies

Apply this comment of James to the case of a business man, for example, who is tempted to take a "short cut" to make some "easy money" in a way not quite in accordance with the law. What is going to determine whether the man goes down in that flood of temptation or not? Many things enter into it, but the largest factor is his habit of daily action or inaction on the truth as he knows it. What light does this throw on the importance of daily decisions even on small matters?

The same things determine a man's ability to meet other trials and emergencies, disappointment and failure, sickness and bereavement. George MacDonald's couplet has truly described the history of thousands of persons:

> "There came a mist and a blinding rain,
> And life was never the same again."

Some great loss comes and a man's courage and, in some cases, his kindliness is swept away in the flood. Others meet the shock of afflictions and losses without giving way to bitterness or allowing the outcome of their lives to be spoiled. The actual practice of truth every day has made

---

[1] James, Psychology, Briefer Course, pp. 147, 148.

it such a reality in their lives that it is a rock foundation in time of storm.

Consider Lincoln's victory over temptation in the light of the scrupulous honesty of all his previous years. When urged to do certain things in order to insure his election to the United States Senate, he answered in words that well deserve a place in the memory of every man and woman, boy and girl: "I am not bound to be elected, but I *am* bound to be true." Honor had been so deeply ingrained into his nature by years of honest living that his character was an unmovable rock. When Martin Luther's opponents were seeking to frighten him out of his position, they told him that the princes of Germany would not rally to his support. They asked him, "Where will you be then?" "Right where I am now," Luther replied calmly, "in the hands of Almighty God." A real faith had made God so much of a reality to him that he was able to meet the crisis without fear.

What experiences test most severely the genuineness of a man's religion?

THE HOUSE ON THE SAND

It must be remembered that in drawing the picture of the man who built a house on the sand Jesus did not have in mind the malicious, but the thoughtless—a much larger class. The man who listens to the teachings of Jesus but who allows them no real control over his actions is the one who has no foundation to his character. He can no more resist the swirl of the severe temptations and trials of life than a squatter's shanty along the Mississippi River bottoms can resist the onset of the spring floods.

Jesus is describing a large class of people here and the solemn warning with which the Sermon on the Mount and this particular parable end, have a close application to the everyday life of every man. It is as direct as the pointed index finger. Suppose some one had come to Jesus, as he went down the mount after the Sermon on the Mount had been delivered, and had said with great enthusiasm, "I enjoyed your sermon very much this morning, Master!" What would Jesus have said? What kind of a look would he have given the one who would give him such a compliment? We do not need to guess what his answer would have been, for this parable is the answer to just such a situation. We know what he said when some one sought to parry the personal thrust of his truth by an empty exclamation. After Jesus had been speaking of duties to the lame, the halt, and the blind, one of the hearers exclaims, gushingly, "Blessed is he that shall eat bread in the kingdom of God." Jesus turned immediately and set forth the cost of discipleship (Luke 14. 15-35). He will not allow his demand for obedience to be lost in sentimentality.

POPULAR SUBSTITUTES FOR ACTION

One very popular substitute for following the teachings of Jesus is to admire them. It is popular because it is so much easier. It is always in good taste to admire Christianity, and it costs nothing. Admiration of this kind is worth just what it costs. Several years ago a plow was sent over to Africa and fell into the possession of a tribe of natives in the interior of the continent. Not knowing what else to do with it they set it up on a pedestal and worshiped it. The plow was designed to strike down deep into the soil and prepare it to produce fruit. To be set up for admiring worship was a perversion of its purpose. So the purpose of the gospel of Jesus is to plow down deep into men's lives and make them fruitful in the largest sense. It is a poor substitute for this to pay to the gospel a few cheap and easy and empty compliments. Dr. Crothers compares the difference which frequently exists between the principles people admire and those they use to two pokers for the fireplace. The fine brass poker in a polished stand is to be looked at. When we really have to do anything to the fire we get out a dingy little black poker which stands somewhere out of sight. So we keep in public view, he says, the beautiful principles we admire and supposedly believe. But when we really have to do anything, we follow some much less attractive principle of action which we keep out of sight. Thus "Love your enemies" is the principle we believe in publicly. "Get even with them," is the principle we privately follow. Does this describe any similar condition in your life? In what respect?

Another substitute for doing the truth is to discuss it. Thus many people who have very pronounced and emphatic views about particular doctrines of Christianity do not show very pronounced or emphatic Christian character. The danger of expending itself in talk is one of the most insidious perils which our religion has to meet. A whole church may come to regard the hearing of two excellent sermons a week as its chief end in life. A Bible class may discuss the teachings of the Bible and let the matter end there. What is your class doing to avoid this danger? What else should a Bible class do?

As another substitute for becoming real disciples of Jesus, many people wish the church well. They patronize it with a few kind words. They say: "Of course I sympathize with the church. I won't join it nor attend it regularly, but I'll give it a little money to support it, and I want my children to go to Sunday school. I think there ought to be a church in the community." Would there ever be a church anywhere if everyone took that attitude? Has that ever been your attitude? Is it now?

"He that hath ears, let him hear," was one of the favorite sayings of Jesus. It singles us out of the crowd and says, "I mean you!" It presses home the question, "Where do you live, on the rock or on the sand?" We cannot tell about others. We have our opinions, no doubt, and too often form judgments on insufficient evidence. But we ought to know about ourselves. Are we satisfied with merely hearing the truth or have we formed the habit of acting on it?

FOR REFLECTION AND DISCUSSION

What light does this parable throw on the importance of habit formation? Which is the harder task, to establish a good habit or to break off a bad one?

Which has had the greater emphasis in religious education, the imparting of information and precept or training in action?

What is the effect of action on truth which has been studied?

What have been the hardest temptations you have had to meet?

Apply this parable to national life. What are some of the dangers which threaten a nation's strength and prosperity? How does a Christian foundation of national life equip it to meet them?

What are the particular or peculiar tests of character in youth? In middle-age?

Can a person receive too much religious exhortation? Under what conditions?

What experiences have been the most frequent causes of the breakdown of religious life and the deterioration of character?

Our coins bear the inscription, "In God we trust." To what extent is our government founded on Christian principles? Our economic system?

CHAPTER V

THE PEARL OF GREAT PRICE.
THE HIDDEN TREASURE

Matthew 13. 44-46

"The Realm of heaven is like treasure hidden in a field; the man who finds it hides it and in his delight goes and sells all he possesses and buys that field.

Again, the Realm of heaven is like a trader in search of fine pearls; when he finds a single pearl of high price, he is off to sell all he possesses and buy it."

THE INNER KINGDOM

THERE is an Oriental fairy story of a tent made of material so delicate that it could be folded up and easily contained in the palm of a man's hand; yet when it was unrolled and set up it would afford shelter for an army of thousands of men. In somewhat the same manner the conception of the kingdom of God seems to expand or contract as Jesus uses it. Sometimes it seems to be the possession of one man. At other times it takes in countless millions in its embrace. It is both a personal good in individual life and a social order for the race. It is too inclusive an ideal to be brought into the limits of a definition. The phrase "the kingdom of God" cannot be understood apart from Jesus' life and character. In all its different manifestations it is an order of life in this present world which corresponds to the ideals and character of Jesus. All that Jesus had to say about the way men ought to live must be included in our idea of what the kingdom of God is. It is the reign of God in the heart and consequently in the organized life of men.

In some of the parables Jesus seems to emphasize the

Kingdom as an outward growth, a social ideal of growing sway. The Mustard Seed and the Leaven are two parables with this emphasis. The Parables of the Treasure and of the Pearl of Great Price emphasize rather the Kingdom as a personal inward possession.

The Noblest Quest

When Jesus likens the Kingdom to buried treasure he strikes a theme which has always had a romantic interest. There is hardly a man who has grown up along the Atlantic coast of the United States who has not as a boy gone out to discover and dig up the buried gold of Captain Kidd. Many of the best-loved stories of youth have had the search or finding of buried treasure as their theme, such as Stevenson's Treasure Island and Poe's The Gold Bug. But while the finding of buried treasure still possesses for our time an unfailing romantic interest, it is something which rarely happens. In Palestine in the time of Christ it happened often. The reason, of course, was that there were no banks and one of the common ways of securing comparative safety for one's treasure was to bury it in a field where its location would be unknown. It frequently happened that a person would die without revealing the place in which his property was buried. Such treasure would be accidentally discovered in time in most cases, and it is to the accidental discovery of the treasure that Jesus compares the finding of the kingdom of God. The main point is that the Kingdom is richer treasure, the finding of which should bring a far deeper thrill of joy than the upturning of buried gold ever brought.

The other comparison which Jesus makes has just as much warm human interest in it. The lure of a great and famous jewel has always exercised a subtle fascination on men's minds. Men have searched and toiled for a lifetime in the hope of making the discovery of a jewel that would make them forever rich. One of the world's famous jewels, a diamond known as the "Star of South Africa," was accidentally found by a shepherd boy on a South African farm. A trader in Hopetown, Van Niekirk, heard of the unusual stone and made a hurried trip to the spot and bought the stone from the boy for five hundred sheep, ten oxen, and a horse. It was found to be a diamond eighty-three and a half carats in weight. A few weeks later Van Niekirk sold the jewel to a Hopetown firm for fifty-six thousand dollars. It was later sold in London for several times that amount. It is to the winning of an unsurpassed jewel of fabulous worth that Jesus compares the winning of the Kingdom. Great as have been the fortunes won by seekers of rare jewels, the man who sets out to realize the kingdom of God in himself is on the nobler quest of a far richer prize.

What Is the Highest Good?

One of the most discussed questions of the ancient world was this: "What is the highest good?" Answers to it are as eagerly sought in the modern world to-day. A man's response to that question is the keystone of his moral system. By the depth and insight of his answer his philosophy of life is judged. But it is not only a question of philosophy. It is an intensely practical question of personal life. It comes to us in this form, "What is the best thing in life which I can get? What is there which, if won, will make life a success; and, if lost, will make it a failure?"

The answers to the question have been many. According to some the highest good in life is pleasure. That was the answer of the Epicurean philosophy of Greece and is the practical answer of vast numbers who make pleasure the ruling passion of their lives. To others it has been power. One of the reasons why Napoleon has exercised such a sway over the imagination of millions of men is that his career embodied the ideal of power which they secretly worship. To others wealth is the highest good. Not many would admit that they considered the acquisition of wealth the chief end in life. But they show their real belief by the fact that they devote their energies to its pursuit. Fame appears to some the highest good of all, sometimes as an ignoble desire for public notice; sometimes as a far higher and more worthy ambition, to make one's name immortal.

Jesus' Answer—"The Kingdom of God"

The parables of the Hidden Treasure and the Pearl of Great Price are Jesus' direct answer to this question. The Kingdom of God is the treasure worth all else, the pearl without a peer. The phrase "the kingdom of God," or "kingdom of Heaven," to use Matthew's translation, was one of large meaning to Jesus. It means the "Reign of God" and the reign of love in the life of the individual and of society. That is made clear in the Lord's Prayer, where the petition "Thy kingdom come" is expanded by adding, "Thy will be done." In other words, the kingdom of heaven is present wherever God's rule is recognized, wherever God's will is done. For us to have the reign of God in our lives means that we have the relationship of loyal and loving sonship to God which Jesus has shown to be possible for us; it means that we are winning a character patterned after his own ideal; it means that we hold as our own Jesus' purpose of making love, service, and brotherhood prevail on the earth.

This, then, is the greatest prize of life, according to Jesus. Was he right? Is there any way of discovering whether he was right or not? What is the price which must be paid for this treasure? Is it really a good bargain, a wise investment, or is the price too high? These are plain questions which crowd on us for an answer.

The Value of Christian Character

The kingdom of God is the highest good possible in any life because—

(1) It satisfies deeper needs of life than anything else can. The possession of Christian character does not affect what a man has, so much as it determines what a man is. A man's first and greatest physical need is the need for health, for physical well-being. Compared to that inner possession, all externals, be they ever so magnificent—clothing, food, houses and lands—are trifling. Character is the health of a man's soul. Deeper than the need of things is the need of a self, a self at harmony with God and sharing his great purposes in filial love and trust and

at harmony with men in good will and brotherhood. Man's
deepest need is expressed in the cry:

> "O for the man to arise in me
> That the man I am may cease to be!"

Jesus' gift of the Kingdom enables a new man to arise,
new in character because new in relationship to God, just
as the earth takes on a new character of beauty in the
spring because it has come into new relationship to the
sun.

The British Weekly a few years ago conducted a ques-
tionnaire among its readers, asking, "What are the things
which have made you happy or unhappy?" Hundreds of
different things were mentioned in the thousands of answers. But they had this striking fact in common. They
ascribed happiness to inner conditions, to the character
and state of the heart rather than to things. Love, friend-
ship, trust, honor, service—these things of the kingdom
of God are the things which make happiness. Make the
same test of the truth yourself: What are the things which
make your happiness?

(2) The Kingdom answers to man's highest aspiration.
Man is more than animal. All the altars and temples of
all the religions of the world are eloquent testimony that
man is a spirit who reaches out after God. The discovery
of God the Father is the greatest event in any man's life.
It completely revolutionizes life. Christ leads men to that
discovery. There have been high moments in the history
of the race when some man has made a great discovery.
We think of Archimedes having just discovered the law of
specific gravity, rushing down the street crying, "Eureka!
Eureka! I have found it!" We think of Columbus pacing
the deck on that October night and the thrill of startled
joy which must have come to him as he saw a light on the
distant shore. We think of Newton in his garden, and of
the wonder that must have taken hold of him as the conception of the law of gravitation flashed into his mind.
But it is a greater thrill of joy which comes into the heart
when a man makes the discovery of God in Christ and
realizes that it is possible for him to receive God into his

life and establish a real fellowship with him. Some one asked Sir James Simpson, the Edinburgh scientist, what he considered his greatest discovery. He replied with great simplicity and humility, "The discovery of Jesus Christ as my Saviour."

(3) The Kingdom is not only a treasure of infinitely finer quality but of infinitely longer duration. External possessions come and go. All the possession a man can be sure of is what he has made of himself. Every one must expect the latter half of life to take on a dwindling character in some respects. The satisfactions of appetite become less and less. Strength decreases. Friends slip away. Unless one can say, as only a Christian can say, "My mind to me a kingdom is," old age or misfortune and loss of property become bitter tragedies. But the Kingdom is eternal treasure. When we become members of the Kingdom, we enter here and now on eternal life. All earthly treasure slips from the nerveless hands of its owner when his last breath is drawn. But the one who has realized in himself the Christian ideal of life has treasure laid up where no thief, not even death, breaks through and steals. Death brings only a new dividend on his investment. It is incorruptible, undefiled, and, even when all else disappears and the soul stands alone, it fades not away.

THE COST OF THE BEST

"It does not take much of a man to be a Christian," some one has truly said, "but it takes all there is of him." That is just the truth which these parables hold. The cost of the best is all that a man has. On no other point was Jesus more explicit or more emphatic than that the Kingdom demands sacrifice. "If any man cometh unto me, and hateth not his own father, and mother, and wife, and children, and brethren, and sisters, yea, and his own life also, he cannot be my disciple" (Luke 14. 26). "If any man would come after me, let him deny himself, and take up his cross, and follow me" (Matt. 16. 24). "If thy right eye causeth thee to stumble, pluck it out, and cast it from thee" (Matt. 5. 29). These are hard sayings. Jesus repeats them again and again. He portrays the

Kingdom as earth's best investment but never once announces that the price is low. It demands all.

To be sure, the Kingdom is a gift. That truth, recovered from oblivion by the Reformation, must never be allowed to become dim. But when we consider the Kingdom as the rule of God, either in one life or in the wide relationship of all men, it is both a gift and a task. It is the gift of an opportunity which we must make a reality by sacrifice and toil. It is like receiving a present of a farm. It is a gift of great value, but without our toil and sacrifice it produces absolutely nothing. So the free gift of God, his Kingdom, produces blessing when we "buy up the opportunity" with sacrifice and toil.

Why should it not be so? Is not the price of highest achievement in any department of life the giving of our best and all of it? Let Goodyear answer for the noble company of inventors. He experimented for weary years with the process of making rubber before he perfected it, putting every penny he had or could raise into it, living often in hunger and selling even his children's school-books and shoes, because it was worth all to him to win the secret. In another field Gibbon worked for twenty years on his History of the Decline and Fall of the Roman Empire. Leonardo da Vinci gave the toil and thought of ten years to the painting of "The Last Supper." What other instances of constant and complete devotion to a task can you mention?

Possession must follow discovery. The merchant who found the pearl sold all he had and bought it. Many people would have been satisfied to spend their lives talking about what a wonderful pearl they had seen; how large it was; how perfectly shaped, and what beautiful, soft luster it had! That is what many Christians are doing—talking about what a wonderful religion Christianity is, instead of living it. Their threadbare testimonies at prayer meeting are the same they gave ten years ago. There is no new Christian achievement in their lives. Christianity can do nothing for us till we give it a place of authority over our lives. Merely talking about it generates as much power as discussing the principles of motion. The rich

young ruler is a classic example of one who discovered the
Kingdom, realized its value, but declined to give his all
for it. Dante calls his action "The Great Refusal." In
what different ways are men making "the great refusal"
to-day, men who are attracted by Jesus, and believe him
to be true, and yet do not follow him? Whose action does
yours resemble most, that of the rich young ruler or of the
merchant seeking pearls?

THE KIND OF SACRIFICE DEMANDED

Each man alone knows what the price of the Kingdom
is to him. Jesus put it in general terms when he said,
"If thy hand cause thee to stumble, cut it off: it is good
for thee to enter into life maimed, rather than having two
hands to go into hell." In concrete terms the cost means
giving up all that prevents God's rule in one's heart. More
positively, it means bringing to him for his use every
faculty and possession. It means seeking with earnest
effort to bring in Christ's order of love, brotherhood, and
service and making it the controlling principle of the organized life of men in our town, our State, our country,
and the whole world. Whenever a man who is a lover of
money renounces his covetousness, when the lover of pleasure or the man under control of appetite conquers the love
of his habitual indulgence, when the proud man and woman
cast pride aside and become humble, when the lazy man
overcomes his love of "slippered ease," when the hard man
becomes a little more human and sympathetic, then each
is selling what he has and buying the Kingdom. Some
habit of years, some cherished companionship, some prejudice, must perhaps be given up before the treasure of the
Kingdom is truly ours. The Kingdom as a social ideal
brings a high cost also. To seek the Kingdom as the ruling
power in the social life of men may mean a willingness to
have profits decrease, to forego luxuries, to have "independence" restricted and the old feeling of selfish irrespon-
sibility disturbed. It will mean the giving up of class prejudice and class feeling—and national prejudices. It will
mean gaining a new habit of cooperation, and all new
habits are hard to establish. But the prize is richly worth

the cost. What has the effort to realize the Kingdom in the relationships of your community ever cost you? What has it cost others?

THE DANGER OF A "CHEAP" RELIGION

This parable sounds a needed warning to-day. We live in a time of comfort and convenience and of toleration, and there is a strong tendency toward cheap and easy religion with few duties attached. People are searching for bargains everywhere else and look for them in religion. The preacher or the sect with a "marked-down" religion to offer at a low cost is popular. Some one has keenly said that there is something radically wrong with the Christian whose favorite song is "I'm glad salvation's free." It is a sign of a far more healthy religion when one sings,

> "Love so amazing, so divine,
> Demands my soul, my life, my all."

Too many people are willing to use Christ only as a convenience and not follow him as a Master. They are Christians on their own terms, up to the point where it profits them in social or business life, but not up to the point where it costs sacrifice. Therefore they never own the treasure.

The Church of Christ is not a social club. It is not a literary society nor a saint's everlasting rest. It is an army moving on the high enterprise of making Jesus Christ known, loved, and obeyed throughout the whole world. Have you enlisted your all?

FOR REFLECTION AND DISCUSSION

What effects will devotion to the Kingdom have on your life?

What arguments would you use in persuading a person to become a follower of Christ? What, actually, does a Christian have in his life which others do not?

How much does it cost to-day to be a Christian? What elements in the cost of becoming a Christian deter most people from being followers of Christ?

What will be the cost of establishing the Kingdom of God in your community? What things must be given up?

Why is the Kingdom of God a higher good than wealth? Why higher than fame? How can the Kingdom be a gift and also something that costs a large price?

Has religion become "too easy"? What are the effects of a religion which costs little or nothing?

What light does this parable throw on the importance of religious education? Do parents, as a rule, place as much emphasis on religious education as on secular education? If not, why not?

Can there be a Christian life which does not incur suffering?

Does your life give the impression that the possession of the Kingdom is a great joy? What influence has a "sour" or gloomy Christian?

CHAPTER VI

THE GOOD SAMARITAN

Luke 10. 25-37

Now a jurist got up to tempt him. "Teacher," he said, "what am I to do to inherit life eternal?" He said to him, "What is written in the law? What do you read there?" He replied, *"You must love the Lord your God with your whole heart, with your whole soul, with your whole strength, and with your whole mind. Also your neighbour as yourself."* "A right answer!" said Jesus; *"do that and you will live."* Anxious to make an excuse for himself, however, he said to Jesus, "But who is my neighbour?" Jesus rejoined, "A man going down from Jerusalem to Jericho fell among robbers who stripped and belaboured him and then went off leaving him half-dead. Now it so chanced that a priest was going down the same road, but on seeing him he went past on the opposite side. So did a Levite who came to the spot; he looked at him but passed on the opposite side. However a Samaritan traveller came to where he was and felt pity when he saw him; he went to him, bound his wounds up, pouring oil and wine into them, mounted him on his own steed, took him to an inn, and attended to him. Next morning he took out a couple of shillings and gave them to the innkeeper, saying, 'Attend to him, and if you are put to any extra expense I will refund you on my way back.' Which of these three men, in your opinion, proved a neighbour to the man who fell among the robbers?" He said, "The man who took pity on him." Jesus said to him, "Then go and do the same."

A Working Model of Love

Lifelike and full of human interest, warm and tender with sympathy and with a plain meaning of universal application, the figure of the Good Samaritan has furnished to all centuries since the time of Christ a working model of what religion should mean in daily life. It has helped the world to remember—what Jesus did not wish men to forget—that religion is social and neighborly. Avoiding all definition and disputation as to who one's neighbor *is,* Jesus presents a beautiful and convincing picture of what the neighborly spirit of love *does.*

"WHO IS MY NEIGHBOR?"

The world owes much to the men who asked questions of Jesus. The questions which were put to him cover the great problems of human life; and our appreciation of the real greatness of Jesus grows as we watch him take his way through these hard questions. Many of them are put with the intention of tripping him, yet he never becomes confused nor evades them, and always reaches the very heart of the matter with an answer which states the truth for all time.

When the lawyer came to Jesus, asking, "What shall I do to inherit eternal life?" he brought one of the great universal questions which have occupied the thought of men in all ages and in all lands. Jesus responded in a way which he often used. He threw the man back on his own resources. He insisted that the questioner help to frame an answer himself. The answer which the lawyer gave showed that he had true religious understanding and appreciated the spirit as well as the letter of the Old Testament law. Jesus, ever eager to commend whenever he met truth and right, warmly approved his answer. Then the lawyer spoiled it, as men often do. He began to think of himself. "Desiring to justify himself," he said to Jesus, "Who is my neighbor?" His question betrayed a narrow and legal interest in the limits to the operation of love. His question was in effect, "How far must I go in showing this love?" Jesus answered indirectly with a story which declared that love does not ask for limits but looks for openings. He showed that he who could quibble about whether a man in need had a claim on him as a neighbor did not have real love in his heart at all. Love finds a neighbor in every one that is in need and can be helped. "Love . . ., like the sun, does not inquire upon what it shall shine, or whom it shall warm, but shines or warms by the very law of its own being" (Trench).

The Men Who Passed By

It was a very common experience for travelers to be robbed and beaten on the Jericho road, so common, in fact, that in Jesus' time it was known as "the red, or bloody, way." It was also a very common thing for priests and Samaritans to be passing along the road. The story was all the more convincing to its first hearers from the life-likeness of its materials.

Probably the first thought that came into the traveler's mind as he saw the priest approaching him was this: "How lucky I am that this is a priest coming along! He is of the same blood as I am, and, more than that, it is his special business to help the unfortunate." He would be far more hopeful on seeing a priest than some alien or heretical Samaritan. Imagine his disappointment at the averted eyes and hurrying steps of the priest as he passed on the other side of the road! The cruelty of the priest was all the more blameworthy because he was bound to this traveler by ties of special obligation, race, and religion.

The traveler would have the same expectations of the Levite who followed the priest. He too was a countryman and a religious official, and he too passed by with not a finger lifted to help. He even emphasized his selfish in-difference by coming near to examine the case closely and raising false hopes of help. The special and peculiar wrong of the priest and Levite is ours when we refuse to acknowledge any special claim or responsibility to a person or a group. What are the particular ties by which you are bound to others and which constitute a claim on you? What is the relation between these special ties and the duty of service to all in need?

"Even as You and I"

How little value there is in a religion without love clearly appears in the parable. It is a living example of the truth uttered by Saint Paul: "If I have the gift of prophecy, and know all mysteries and all knowledge; and if I have all faith, so as to remove mountains, but have not love, I am nothing." Without any question both the priest

and the Levite could have told exactly what passages in
the Old Testament covered the case. The priest, at least,
could doubtless have quoted accurately every injunction
to mercy to be found in the whole of the Law and the
Prophets, and there are hundreds of them. But while they
knew the law in the matter, they were not familiar with
the deed. Confronted by a concrete case of actual desperate
need, they hurried on, muttering perhaps a feeble and useless, "Too bad!" Yet the Samaritan, who probably did
not know as much law, knew how to do the loving act.
"Love is the fulfilment of the law," whether we know the
law or not. Have you had any similar experience, in that
people from whom help might be expected fail, while those
from whom nothing is expected respond?

Our Shallow Excuses: "Too Busy"

There was only one method which was adequate to deal
with the need of this wounded traveler—immediate personal service. That the priest and Levite failed to give.
Their passing by is typical of many ways of "passing by
on the other side," when men are confronted with human
need to-day. People "pass by" because they are "too busy."
This was doubtless one reason why the priest and Levite
hurried on. Though they were sorry for the poor fellow
by the side of the road, engagements made it impossible
for them to stop. And so the procession hurries on to-day,
"too busy" to upset their plans, or miss their engagements,
in order to help unfortunates, the handicapped, the
wronged. How many men know little or nothing of "how
the other half lives" in their own town, perhaps not ten
blocks away! How many do not care! What is this but
passing by on the other side? How much do you know
about the social conditions of your town? How many
times during the last year have you answered "Too busy"
to appeals for work for the church or for community betterment? Perchance the priest and the Levite were preoccupied with "religious work." They did not realize that
the most holy and religious task to which they could give
themselves just then was to bind up the wounds of this
suffering man. In the routine of religious observances they

had lost their sense of values and had come to regard ceremony as being more important than mercy (see Matt. 23. 23), a condition which has developed again and again in the history of individuals and of churches. As one has said of this priest, "His position had hardened on him like a shell." What examples can you give of religious persons or institutions becoming indifferent to human misery and needs? How does it come about? How can it be prevented?

"IT'S NOT MY BUSINESS"

The priest and Levite may have felt that it was not their business to stop and help. They could easily think of others whose business it was rather than theirs. They might be willing to report the case to a Travelers' Aid Society, but beyond that they were not concerned. This is an easy and ready way of evading calls for help. Millions of people use it every day. Yet such an attitude always shows an utter lack of the Christian spirit of love. All through his teachings, and supremely in this parable, Jesus insisted that all human need is our business to the extent of our power. That is just what the kingdom of God on earth means: that men shall recognize each other as brothers and care for their brothers' welfare and need. With this truth of Jesus in mind, consider some of the duties which may be your particular business: protection of life and property, protection of health, protection of morals, religious education, protection of women and children from exploitation, care of the sick, the delinquent, the criminal, provision of safe and wholesome recreation. Which of these matters are you making your business? If you are not concerned with any of them, how do you differ from the priest and Levite?

"SAFETY FIRST"

We may be sure that the priest and Levite did not regard themselves as heartless monsters. They had their ready excuses which they put to themselves for not giving any aid, "even as you and I." But the very fact that the excuses were made showed the absence of real compassion.

For true sympathy never looks for excuses. One excuse
was danger. They could easily reason that the robbers
must still be near. It was safer to hurry on, and that is
one large reason why there are so many like the priest and
Levite in the world. No one can be very useful who, in a
narrow sense, makes his motto "Safety first." Some men
have refused to sign a petition against a saloon because
it would hurt their business. They see the suffering caused
by the saloon but pass by on the other side. Others have
been afraid to oppose a corrupt political ring because of
"influence." What hindrances to social betterment exist
in your town?

"It's no Use"

A frequent reason for not helping is because people say
complacently, "It's no use." Possibly the priest thought
the traveler was beyond help. It saves so much trouble
to decide that there is no need for our help. We rid ourselves of the task of helping some family to get on its feet,
by saying, "It's no use"; people oppose prison reform by
saying, "It's no use," and regard humanitarian reformers
as crackbrained enthusiasts; they will not work for the
abolition of poverty because "it's no use." This easy way
out of it is usually a lie. Men long endured the scourge
of smallpox and yellow fever and a hundred preventible
ills because it was thought no use to attempt a cure till
some one demonstrated that it could be done. How is the
"no use" argument applied to missions, to prohibition, to
peace propaganda, to a living wage? Have you ever used
it yourself? Beware of ready excuses! There is no surer
sign of deterioration of moral character.

The Good Neighbor

The Good Samaritan sets the obvious in Christianity
clearly before our eyes. It is an important service, for,
strange as it may seem, it is the plain, elementary, obvious
aspects of Christianity which are frequently forgotten.
Christianity is more than helpfulness, but it must include
that. No orthodoxy of opinion or zeal in propaganda can
make up for a moment for the lack of love. The very

essence of Christianity consists in the willingness to do just what the Good Samaritan did—share some advantage that is ours with some one who needs it. This is what Paul means when he pleads, "Have this mind in you which was also in Christ Jesus." The man to whom Jesus points with the injunction "Go, and do thou likewise" is well worthy of study. He is a model of love in action.

PERSONAL SERVICE

The service of the Good Samaritan was personal. And in no respect is he more worthy of eternal emulation than in that. He got down from his horse and gave himself to the man's needs. This is worth noting in these days when so many things are done through organizations and committees. Organization is so great a help in all good work that there has grown up a pathetic faith that all that is necessary to overcome an evil is to form an organization, appoint committees, and deal with it impersonally. Dr. Charles R. Brown says, keenly: "This story would have been very different if the Samaritan had seen the trouble and said, 'When I reach home I must send a check to the Relief Corps for Wounded Travelers'; or if he had simply determined to get a ringing resolution passed at the next meeting of the association, denouncing 'these Bedouin atrocities'; or if he had consumed all his philanthropic zeal in writing 'an open letter' to the paper on the laxity of police regulations on the road between Jerusalem and Jericho. In the meantime, the poor, wounded, half-dead traveler would have been dead altogether. What the Good Samaritan did was to take personal care of the needy man; after that the check, the open letter, the resolutions might be very well."

Some one has wittily said that an American's remedy for any wrong is to appoint a committee. The personal touch gives way to officious inquiry. It is this tendency which has given rise to the description,

> "Organized charity, scrimped and iced
> In the name of a cautious, statistical Christ."

Organized charity is absolutely necessary, but it need not

become hard and unsympathetic. It needs much personal contact to save it. Its main reliance to-day is not on paid secretaries, but on the "friendly visitor," an unpaid voluntary worker who takes a real interest in people, rather than a professional interest in "cases." Many people are much more ready to discuss the immigration problem than to care for an immigrant on the next block. Contrast with this attitude the time and attention which Jesus gave to individuals. Notice the beginning of this very parable— "a certain man." When Jesus talks about love it is always in the concrete—love to some particular people. It is easy to love men when that means only a vague feeling of good will to humanity in general. Such a feeling is worth little or nothing. An illustration of this is found in the people who profess to believe in the brotherhood of man, but who call some of those who make up that brotherhood "dagos" and "sheenies" and "niggers." Religion becomes easy and useless just in proportion as it grows vague.

The Good Samaritan's help was not only personal, it was self-sacrificing. Many people are willing to play the Good Samaritan without the oil and two pence. Much of our giving stops this side of the point where it hurts or causes us to give up something. The Samaritan gave of his time, for he was undoubtedly on a business journey. He gave of his money and goods, and it may well have meant some privation to himself. He gave his service,— getting down from his beast and lifting up the wounded man. His service was thorough. He did not leave his task of rescue half done, with the pious hope that the man would "get along all right," or the vague request to "write me if I can do anything for you." He "saw it through," and in doing so he is a model for Christian effort. Much effort is lost because it is scattered too much. Dr. Cabot says that Paul's "this one thing I do" has become "these forty things I dabble in."

"Go, and Do Thou Likewise"

There is an electric quality about Jesus' command at the end of the parable. The lawyer could not by any means mistake the pointed personal application to himself which Jesus made. Neither can any of us. We must ask ourselves: "Am I doing likewise? How hard am I trying to do likewise?"

Where in these days do you find the counterpart of this poor, half-dead traveler? It may not be some one in actual physical distress. Perhaps it is an unfortunate friend who is having a hard time to get along or some one wounded and robbed by heredity, whom our advantage can help. We cannot be indifferent to the cause of the unprivileged, the underpaid, the unfortunate without crossing over to the other side of the Jericho road with the priest and Levite.

One of our greatest dangers to-day is that of living a life so sheltered and so busy that we never see the man in need. It was said of Goethe that "he kept well out of sight of stripped and wounded and half-dead men." He found such things unpleasant and so lived his life in sheltered places. It is surprising how easy it is to live out of sight of suffering even in a great city where there is so much. One can live in a "fine" section of town, move among "nice" people, belong to a pleasant church, and never feel the twinge of pain or misery or see the anguish of pain or the squalor of poverty. Because it does not come on our daily beaten track we forget that it exists. And in that sheltered, thoughtless ease lies the chief reason that the world still contains after two thousand years of Christ so much unrelieved pain and want.

FOR REFLECTION AND DISCUSSION

In what respects are the following classes of the community like the traveler who was robbed and beaten: the immigrant, the poor, the sick, the defective, the ignorant? How can we act the part of the Good Samaritan to these classes?

Suppose the Good Samaritan had come along the road when the robbers were just beginning to attack the traveler. What would have been his duty then? How does your answer apply to the present-day movement for the prevention of evil?

What are the most urgent needs of your community? What are the most neglected classes?

What responsibility has the church to the community outside its doors? What can the church as an organization do to put the Christian spirit into legislation?

How does the Christian treatment of the immigrant help to establish brotherly international relations?

What are the most dangerous forms of organized evil today?

How can we make the response to need habitual?

What has been the effect of Christianity on the feeling of pity?

What more than emotion does Jesus mean by love?

CHAPTER VII

THE TEN VIRGINS

Matthew 25. 1-13

"Then shall the Realm of heaven be compared to ten
maidens who took their lamps and went out to meet the
bridegroom and the bride. Five of them were stupid and
five were sensible. For although the stupid took their lamps,
they took no oil with them, whereas the sensible took oil
in their vessels as well as their lamps. As the bridegroom
was long of coming, they all grew drowsy and went to sleep.
But at midnight the cry arose, 'Here is the bridegroom! Come
out to meet him!' Then all the maidens rose and trimmed
their lamps. The stupid said to the sensible, 'Give us some
of your oil, for our lamps are going out.' But the sensible
replied, 'No, there may not be enough for us and for you.
Better go to the dealers and buy for yourselves.' Now while
they were away buying oil, the bridegroom arrived; those
maidens who were ready accompanied him to the marriage-
banquet, and the door was shut. Afterwards the rest of the
maidens came and said, 'Oh sir, oh sir, open the door for us!'
but he replied, 'I tell you frankly, I do not know you.'
Keep on the watch then, for you know neither the day nor
the hour."

THE opening verses of the 24th chapter of Matthew give
the occasion of this parable, which occurs, with two others,
in the 25th chapter. On being shown the wonders of the
temple at Jerusalem, Jesus tells his disciples that a time
will come when one stone shall not be left upon another.
Later, on the Mount of Olives, when the opportunity of
private conversation has come, they ask him eagerly, "When
shall these things be?" Naturally, they are very anxious
to learn the exact date of the establishment of the kingdom
of heaven on earth. The answer Jesus gives to this question occupies two whole chapters, Matthew 24 and 25, and
includes three parables.

The essence of Jesus' answer is this: "Watch therefore,

for ye know not the day nor the hour." The three parables in Matthew 25 set forth what Jesus meant by "watch." The Parable of the Ten Virgins stresses the necessity for preparation. In the Parable of the Talents the need of fidelity is urged. In the Parable of the Last Judgment it is the duty of love which is set forth.

A GRIPPING STORY

In sheer interest as a dramatic story scarcely any of the parables surpasses that of the Ten Virgins. Try to tell it in any other words, and you will discover how much weaker your version or that of anyone else is than the original. Its rapid movement, the startling suddenness of the midnight cry, the haste of the surprised sleepers, and the weird pathos of those shut out from the warm glow of the banquet room—all these elements make it an intensely interesting story and have given it a firm hold on the Christian imagination.

It is as the vehicles of spiritual truth, however, that the parables continue of interest to the world. And while probably no parable has suffered more than this one from extravagances of interpretation and the finding of ingenious meanings in every minor detail, nevertheless, if we take its broad meanings, it is exceedingly plain and simple and comes very close home to the everyday problems of living for all men.

THE SUPREME EMERGENCY

The supreme emergency treated in this parable is the coming of the kingdom of heaven. Jesus says that it will be unexpected, but he does not say how soon it will come. Readiness and patience are both needed. How much need there was for just this teaching is clearly shown by the history of the early church, which did not thoroughly learn this lesson of the tarrying kingdom. They expected the second coming of Christ very soon and were often disappointed. They had to realize over and over again the truth of Jesus' words, "The end is not yet."

There are many Christian people who are greatly interested in the time and the exact details of the second coming of Christ. What light does this parable throw on the profitableness of all attempts to figure out the date and the manner of the coming of Christ? Does it not urge the duty of readiness by life and service rather than curiosity as to times and seasons? There are, in general, two kinds of watchfulness. They may be illustrated by a fisherman's wife, whose husband is expected back from the sea. She can either spend all her time down on the dock looking through a telescope or she can busy herself preparing for his needs when he returns. Which kind of watchfulness do you think is the better illustration of wise Christian conduct?

Are you accustomed to think of the coming of Christ as far away in a dim future? Have you ever thought of it as something that is going on every day, that is actually happening in the present? Think for a moment of that conception of it. The progressive coming of the Christ and his kingdom in the daily expansion of his rule over the hearts and lives of men and the increasing knowledge and obedience to him on the part of millions of people is a very real daily "coming" of Christ. Is not Christ coming to China, to India, to America, in a growing sense every year? Does he not "come again" in every new life given over to the control of his spirit? The conviction that Christ is actually coming to-day in larger measure as the ruler of men's hearts, and so of the world, is a strong incentive to active daily service. If we consider the second coming of Christ as his progressive coming every day in a wider lordship over men's lives, is it possible for us to hasten that coming by our action? In what ways? What are you doing now to hasten the establishment of the kingdom of God?

DEFICIENT GOODNESS

The neglect of the foolish virgins represents a failure to prepare for the coming of the Kingdom. As we think of them in that light, several types of conduct, likewise hindrances to the advance of the Kingdom, come readily to mind.

Here the foolish virgins resemble closely the soil which

had no depth of earth in the Parable of the Sower and the foolish builder who built on sand. Mark Twain tells of steamboats on the Mississippi which exhausted all their steam in blowing the whistle. Have you ever seen emotional religion which had little effect on conduct? What effect does indulgence in religious emotion, when it does not result in practical action, have on character? Sentiment without sacrifice is another form of emotion not backed up by action. Have you ever known people who liked sermons which touched the feelings, but who never translated feeling into action? There can be no greater mistake in any enterprise of life, particularly of the religious life, than to suppose that a few warm excited feelings will carry one through triumphantly to the end and take the place of a long course of patience and self-denial. Enthusiasm and emotion, though good, are of little value when not backed up by perseverance. Principles and habits must supplement feelings in every important undertaking. How can a good emotion or feeling become a habit?

Church activity or church membership without righteousness is another kind of "foolish virgin goodness" which counts for nothing. Ecclesiastical machinery is simply the form without life, without vital goodness. Church membership is a good expression of righteousness. It is a poor substitute for it.

The Peril of Superficiality

The parable makes clear, then, the danger of superficiality, the serious possibility that our religious life may consist mainly of outward observances and pretensions, having very little core of genuine faith and conviction. Those who lay out their scheme of life so that it may please the eye of men rather than Him that "seeth in secret," make the perilous mistake of the foolish virgins in being more careful of the outward than the inward. Indeed, the advance of civilization in convenience and complexity increases the tendency toward superficiality in many departments of life in social intercourse and education, for instance. What forces to-day are causing this? How about pressure on time? The prevalence of imitation? The worship of "success" as an ideal of life? What effect do these have on the thoroughness and vitality of religious life?

The failure of the foolish virgins lay in neglect. What forms of neglect in our religious life are most common? Can a person's religious life be kept strong and vigorous without prayer? Consider the place prayer occupied in the life of Jesus as a preparation for temptation and service. In that light how large a place does it occupy in your life? Consider meditation and obedience. Can these be safely neglected?

THE TEST OF EMERGENCY

The parable also vividly portrays the truth that emergency tests character. Until the bridegroom came the difference between the virgins was not evident. The sudden midnight call divided them into two classes—the prepared and the neglectful. So a crisis or emergency reveals what we really are. When we realize that this tested character is a gradual growth, we know that there are no ordinary or unimportant days. "As we become permanent drunkards by so many separate drinks, so we become saints in the moral world, and authorities and experts in practical and scientific spheres, by so many separate acts and hours of work. Let no youth have any anxiety about the upshot of his education, whatever the line of it may be. If he keep faithfully busy each hour of the working day, he may safely leave the final result to itself. He can with perfect certainty count on waking up some fine morning to find himself one of the competent ones of his generation, in whatever pursuit he may have singled out."[1] How would this truth apply directly to the religious life? How does it act as an encouragement to live each day earnestly and zealously?

What are the great emergencies of life which do come or may come to all men and for which we must prepare? How swiftly the common emergencies of life come! The death of a loved one, financial loss, sickness—these and many other crises come upon us as suddenly as the midnight

[1] James, Psychology, Briefer Course, p. 150.

cry, "Behold, the bridegroom cometh!" How many of the following emergencies are common to the lives of most people?—temptations of appetite, of pride, envy, carelessness, laziness; the discouragement of failure or poverty; the moral dangers of success; sickness and invalidism; bereavement; financial loss; disappointed ambition. Which of the above have you faced? How can we prepare for any of these?

TO-DAY'S EMERGENCY

The opportunity for action which shall prepare for the coming of the Kingdom on earth was never larger than to-day. Never was the time more truly epoch-making than the days in which we live. A thoughtful student of affairs said recently, "I had rather be living in the next ten years than in any other decade of human history." It was his conviction that the events transpiring were of more importance and the opportunities for influence larger than ever before. For the great world war is making a new world. Old habits and customs of life and thought have been broken up never again to be reestablished. Think of the opportunity presented for the advancement of the Kingdom among men by the following tendencies of the war: the enlarging of the horizon of men's minds through new experiences and the growth of international spirit, thus preparing for the Kingdom's ideal of the common good of all; the new reality to the religious faith of millions; the growing hatred of war, deeper than ever before, and the determination that it must cease; the breaking down of barriers of class and caste, the revival of the spirit of unselfishness, fidelity, and sacrifice. All these and many more results make the possibility of reorganizing the life of the nations on a new, sounder, and higher foundation politically, socially, and religiously. Are we, the followers of Christ, ready for this marvelous coming of the Kingdom in our own day? Is our faith strong enough, our vision broad enough to seize the opportunity, so that the generation of reconstruction following the great war may see the greatest advancement of vital Christianity the world has ever known? It demands activity along many lines, promoting international sympathy and enforcing peace, making the social and industrial relations of men Christian in fact as well as in name, strategic advances in the missionary enterprise, securing an adequate place for religious education in the nation's life, drawing the branches of the Christian Church into a working federation presenting a united front in all endeavor. All these to-day are a glorious possibility. What will you do to make them a reality?

CHARACTER CANNOT BE BORROWED

It was one of the truths which were recovered from neglect by the Protestant Reformation that character cannot be borrowed. No merit from another person's acts, his faithfulness, or his service can pass to us. The foolish virgins could not borrow oil from the wise; they must buy for themselves. This was not due, in the story, to arbitrary hard-heartedness on the part of the wise virgins. They were no doubt sorry for the foolish ones. Their refusal indicated a lack of power to give. Personal reserves of spirit and character cannot be transferred in any immediate and easy way. It is impossible for one person to impart to another the spiritual power which comes from frequent communion with God and continued practice of his will. No religious person can give of his character; he can only tell how it may be obtained—no more than a firm-muscled, broad-shouldered athlete can give his strength to an invalid.

Think for a moment of the many modern ways in which this old mistake of the foolish virgins is made. Have you ever heard this bit of doggerel?—

> "In the world's broad field of battle,
> In the bivouac of life,
> You will find the average layman
> Represented by his wife."

We smile at it, but does it not stand for the attitude of many men toward the church and the tasks of the kingdom of God? What preparation for his life's needs and tests will his wife's religious experience and service make for a man? W. M. Taylor says, "We give so much to each other and receive so much from each other in common life, that we are apt to suppose that it is possible in moral things, as well as secular." But our hardest battles must be fought alone, and the only strength available is that inner character which we have actually won for ourselves. Think of the lonely personal battles in the Bible, such as Joseph's resistance of temptation, Moses' choice of God's people, Job's struggle with despair, Jesus' temptation. Remember this; there will come times to you when you will desperately need courage to perform duty, patience under pain, comfort in sorrow. How is your present life preparing you to meet these crises successfully?

Too Late!

There is a tragic sadness at the end of this parable. The picture with which it closes is unforgetable—the bright gleaming lights of the marriage feast, the warmth and fellowship within, the plea of the late comers outside the shut door, and then the stern forbidding words, "I know you not."

Tennyson has expressed very vividly the pathos of the scene:

> "Late, late, so late! and dark the night and chill!
> Late, late, so late! but we can enter still.
>   'Too late, too late! ye cannot enter now!'
>
> "No light had we; for that we do repent,
> And learning this, the Bridegroom will relent.
>   'Too late, too late! ye cannot enter now.'
>
> "No light! so late! and dark and chill the night—
> Oh let us in, that we may find the light.
>   'Too late, too late! ye cannot enter now.'"

What is the application of this tragic story of Jesus to our everyday life? Let us not miss one primary meaning. Death, which comes to every man, is one time when it is "too late." It is too late then to put good intentions into actions, to rectify past wrongs, to give of our strength and time to the needs of men and women. In getting away from morbid thinking about death, have not multitudes of people put the thought of death entirely away from them, with the result that a carelessness has taken the place of a serious urgency in connection with the duties of life? Recall how strongly Jesus felt that his work must be done quickly while opportunity was ripe—"I must work the works of him that sent me while it is yet day, for the night cometh when no man can work." You have your life insured because it is uncertain. Should not the same reason cause you to give your best and utmost service to the kingdom of God every day?

The foolish virgins were not the victims of a relentless and unforgiving friend. Their exclusion represents, rather, the solemn truth that opportunities pass and can never come again. Certain doors shut, never to open again. There may come a time when character can no longer be developed, when the desire for holiness shall cease and the capacity for moral attainment be lost. Every day when we neglect to cultivate the true life in our souls, that life becomes the more difficult to obtain. Character tends to crystallize. God is still ready to forgive men, but they may so habituate themselves to sin that they do not desire or seek forgiveness. Have you ever known anyone whose capacity for moral development seemed completely lost? What other doors of opportunity and privilege do men shut upon themselves by neglect?

The world-wide opportunity of the Kingdom to-day, for instance, is a fleeting one. It cannot possibly be the same for a number of years. If the church is to avail herself of the new religious interest and faith, it must do so now by presenting a religion vital enough to command allegiance. The strategic moment of presenting Christianity as a religion to nations whose long-established faith is crumbling away must be seized immediately. Ten years from now the present opportunity will be gone. How can you help Christian forces to take advantage of the opportunity?

FOR REFLECTION AND DISCUSSION

In what sense is Christ coming to each of us every day?
Which is the severer test of character, poverty or wealth?
Give some illustrations of the necessity for backing up

emotions by principles and habits in reference to benevolence, patriotism, worship.

Can you give any examples of great leaders who were unconsciously prepared for large opportunities by daily fulfilment of obscure and ordinary tasks?

What can we do for one another in our religious life, and what must every man do for himself?

Are most acts due to impulse at the time or to habit?

Are as many failures in business due to lack of ability as to lack of perseverance?   In the Christian life?

In what order would you rank the Parables of Jesus according to their interest as stories?

CHAPTER VIII

THE UNMERCIFUL SERVANT

Matthew 18. 23-35

Then Peter came up and said to him, "Lord, how often is my brother to sin against me and be forgiven? Up to seven times?" Jesus said to him, "Seven times? I say, seventy times seven! That is why the Realm of heaven may be compared to a king who resolved to settle accounts with his servants. When he began the settlement, a debtor was brought in who owed him three million pounds; as he was unable to pay, his master ordered him to be sold, along with his wife and children and all he had, in payment of the sum. So the servant fell down and prayed him, 'Have patience with me, and I will pay you it all.' And out of pity for that servant his master released him and discharged his debt. But as that servant went away, he met one of his fellow-servants who owed him twenty pounds, and seizing him by the throat he said, 'Pay your debt!' So his fellow-servant fell down and implored him, saying, 'Have patience with me, and I will pay you.' But he refused; he went and had him thrown into prison, till he should pay the debt. Now when his fellow-servants saw what had happened they were greatly distressed, and they went and explained to their master all that had happened. Then his master summoned him and said, 'You scoundrel of a servant! I discharged all that debt for you, because you implored me. Ought you not to have had mercy on your fellow-servant, as I had on you?' And in hot anger his master handed him over to the torturers, till he should pay him all the debt. My Father will do the same to you unless you each forgive your brother from the heart."

Love Versus Arithmetic

It is small wonder that as Jesus endeavored to substitute for the hard-and-fast legalism of the Judaism of his time a religion whose center and soul was an active love, he should have found it a slow process. Even those who knew him best and had been with him most were slow to under-

75

stand the vast difference between the new teaching he
brought and the old system of rules under which they had
lived. We have seen that the Parable of the Good Samaritan was called forth by one who wished for mathematical
information. He wished to know just *how far* love would
have to extend. Jesus' answer was not mathematical but
spiritual, that real love had no limits and extended far
enough to cover every case of need. Peter comes to Jesus
with a similar question. *"How many times,"* he asks,
"must I forgive my brother?" There is the same mistaken
interest in exact rules and the same mistaken feeling of
compulsion in Peter's question that there was in that of
the lawyer. Jesus gives him an answer similar to that
given to the lawyer by the Parable of the Good Samaritan.
The whole idea of "how many times" in connection with
forgiveness was utterly wrong. In the story of the Unmerciful Servant Jesus declared that whoever had the
spirit which a child of God ought to have, and who realized
the extent of God's mercy to him, could never think that
it was possible for him to be too forgiving.

When Peter asked if he should forgive his brother seven
times, he no doubt thought himself generous to an extreme,
for he had more than doubled the number of times commonly held by the Jews to be necessary to forgive an
offender. "Forgive three times but not the fourth" was
the common rule justified by the supposed meaning of
Amos 1. 3: "For three transgressions of Damascus, yea,
for four, I will not turn away the punishment thereof,"
and Job 33. 29:

> "Lo, all these things doth God work,
>   Twice, *yea,* thrice, with a man,
>   To bring back his soul from the pit."

But even though seven was a large advance over three,
Peter's question showed that he still missed the spirit of
Christ's teaching. The parable shows that it was not a
mere increase of number of times which Jesus demanded,
but an entirely different spirit, in which there should be
no thought whatever of retaliation, no lurking idea that
one had a right to withhold forgiveness.

The Sin of the Unforgiving Spirit

The most astonishing thing in this parable is its central point, that to cherish an unforgiving spirit is sin. It was an astonishing teaching at that time. To be unforgiving was not regarded as an offense, certainly not as a grave sin. The teaching is to-day just as capable of creating a revolution when carried out into practical daily life. "It is easy enough to accept dead truths or blunt ones," and it is easy enough to believe in a vague, general way that a forgiving disposition is a fine thing. Most people do. But actually to believe that to have a harsh, unforgiving disposition, to cherish a grudge, or a desire to "get even," to be mean and unmerciful or stern and hard, is sin, as truly as any other kind of sin can be, is quite a different thing. If such a working conviction controlled all men, it would entirely change life about us. But that is just exactly what this parable reveals. The enormity of the guilt of the man who carries an unmerciful spirit out into his relations with men is vividly flashed forth in the story of the servant, a collector of taxes or some such high official, who owed an amount of about twelve million dollars and who had it graciously forgiven because he could not pay it, but who refused even to grant an extension of time on a debt of seventeen dollars due to himself and threw his debtor into prison. Then we read that the lord of that servant was angry and cast him into jail for life, an action which clearly indicates how great a sin an unmerciful spirit is in God's sight. Forgiveness and mercy in our relations with each other are not matters of choice, but of necessity. We never have any right to refuse forgiveness, but, in view of the infinite degree of mercy we have all received from God, we have the duty of extending it.

No teaching touches life more nearly at its center than this concerning the necessity of the merciful forgiving spirit. Its field of operation is the busy daily round of trade, of the thronged market place, of social life. The affronts we daily receive, the pressure of competition, the intended injuries and unconscious slights—these things endlessly repeated make an enormous drain on a man's

fund of good will, his evenness of disposition, his readiness
to forgive. How is he to meet them? How is he to keep
in the full stream of crowded life and still retain the
merciful nature with no place for retaliation, which must
characterize the member of the kingdom of God?

"Heavenly Harmonies for Earthly Living"

The same law of gravitation which holds the planets in
poise as they swing in their courses holds the little grain
of dust floating in the air in position as well. All through
his life Jesus emphasizes the truth that the principles
which control the action of God are the principles which
should control the action of his children. He here emphasizes that truth in respect to forgiveness. "Freely ye have
received, freely give"—that is the principle. The unbought
divine forgiveness of God is a "heavenly harmony for
earthly living."

Human actions are to be truly seen and weighed only
when set against a divine background. Thoughtless in-
gratitude appears in its true character only when set
against divine bounty. An unforgiving spirit in men is
seen at its true guilt when contrasted with the forgiving
love of God. It is just that divine background of mercy
by which every man's life must be judged which this parable
shows us. The forgiveness of sins on the part of God is
a free gift of boundless measure. That is represented by
the immense size of the servant's debt. He could never
have paid it, even though he did boastfully promise to pay
all. Release from the debt could never have been purchased by any service of his. If he does not serve in
prison all his days, it is simply by the free grace of his
Lord.

The Unmerciful Servant—United States Edition

The effect of this mercy of God toward men ought to be
to arouse in them a magnanimous and merciful spirit
toward their fellow men. Indeed, such has been the effect
historically, and it is so to-day. The Christian revelation
of God has been the great fountain head of the stream
of mercy, humanity, and forgiveness which is blessing the

world to-day. Part of the Christian appeal for mercy has been very beautifully expressed by Shakespeare in the words of Portia in the Merchant of Venice,

> "Earthly power doth then show likest God's
> When mercy seasons justice. Therefore, Jew,
> Though justice be thy plea, consider this—
> That in the course of justice none of us
> Should see salvation. We do pray for mercy;
> And that same prayer doth teach us all to render
> The deeds of mercy."

Yet there is still to-day a searching truth and timeliness to the parable. Consider the following common cases familiar to all of us. Here is a member of Christ's church who has not been "on speaking terms" with one of his neighbors for a long time but has harbored unforgiving resentment against him for years. Perhaps he even extends his unforgiving aversion to all the members of his neighbor's family. Does not almost every community have some such case of "hard feeling"? How about the man who is simply known as "shrewd," hard as flint, close-fisted, "a bad man to hold a mortgage against you"? Isn't he an "unmerciful servant"? Take the man who has had many strong safeguards on the way of life—good heredity and training and circumstances and who is stern and severe in his judgment of others who have not had all these advantages, and is quick to call them "worthless." Are we not all "unmerciful servants" when we form unsympathetic estimates of the foreigners in the United States, forgetting both the handicap many of them have had and the exceptional advantages we have had? Have we not, as members of the state, been guilty of the same kind of action as the unmerciful servant, when we commit offenders to jail and give them no real opportunity to reform? The sin of the unmerciful spirit appears to be particularly shameful when it is contrasted with the mercy shown to the one committing it by his fellows. Take the all too common case of a business man who adopts an entirely different attitude to his debtors and creditors. To the creditors he is pleading for rebates, extensions of time, and receiving them; to his debtors he is pushing collections to the very limit, making

no extension of time and taking no excuses. Or take a
man whose irascible temper is a sore trial to his family and
friends. They have borne with him patiently. Yet he
is easily irritated with the shortcomings of others and does
not extend to them the patient charity which he has received all his life. "Think over all that people have had to
endure in you; remember the patience and forgiveness of
your parents, the way your friends have overlooked your
blunders and ill nature; consider how your hope of any
chance to retrieve past mistakes in your moral life rests
on God's mercy and willingness to pardon. Then think
how mean it is to cherish grudges against those who wrong
you" (Fosdick).

"The High Cost of Hating"

By cherishing an unforgiving spirit we shut out the possibility of God's *forgiveness*. In the quaint language of
Lord Herbert, "He who cannot forgive others breaks the
bridge over which he must pass." An unforgiving Christian is a contradiction in terms. Unwillingness on our part
to forgive is evidence that we have not been forgiven by
God, according to the plain words of Jesus: "If ye forgive
not men their trespasses, neither will your Father forgive
your trespasses."

The mercy we show to others is to be the measure of the
mercy we ask of God. Augustus Hare says: "Conceive an
unforgiving man praying to God Most High to forgive him
his debts as he forgives his debtors. . . . 'Deal with me,
I beseech thee, even as I deal with my neighbor. He hath
not offended me one tenth, one hundredth part as much as
I have offended thee; but he has offended me very griev-
ously, and I cannot forgive him. . . . I remember and
treasure up every little trifle which shows how badly he has
behaved toward me. Deal with me, I beseech thee, O Lord,
as I deal with him.' . . . Is not the very sound of it
enough to make one's blood run cold? Yet this is just
the prayer which the unforgiving man offers up, every
time he repeats the Lord's Prayer!" Have you ever
thought of the Lord's Prayer in this light? Can you expect
forgiveness while you refuse to grant it?

By an unforgiving spirit we shut out the possibility of *happiness*. Happiness depends far more on the quietness and peace of a man's spirit than on any external conditions whatever. No one can carry a feeling of unrelenting bitterness against another without paying a heavy price for it in the disturbed content of his own heart. Can you give out of your own experience any of the effects of carrying an unforgiving animosity toward anyone? Have you observed its effects on another person? What are they? Abraham Lincoln said, "No man resolved to make the most of himself can spare the time for personal contention. Still less can he afford to take all the consequences, including the vitiating of his temper and loss of self-control."

An unforgiving spirit shuts the door upon the highest *character*. An unforgiving man cannot have a character which resembles that of God or live in fellowship with him. Ask yourself this question honestly: What kind of a memory have I? Is it one that retains the slights and injuries which have been done to me, and reflections which have been made on me? Or does it act like a sieve and allow those injuries to pass on, retaining rather a sharp impression of the benefits conferred on me and kindnesses done? Everyone creates his own memory in this respect. Which kind have you created?

How to Acquire a Merciful Spirit

The unmerciful servant had little realization of the greatness of his debt, or he could never have so violently pressed his claim for seventeen dollars when he had just been forgiven a debt of twelve millions. *The surest means of acquiring a forgiving spirit is to realize vividly the greatness of God's forgiving mercy to us.* Real honest knowledge of self is essential if we are to realize our debt to the forgiveness of God. Such knowledge is rare. The man who has a keen sense of his own shortcomings and defects will be more lenient to others. It is pride which is inexorable in its hard judgments. Men fail to see themselves as they really are because they measure themselves by custom and the average standards that prevail in the community. Or, worse still and quite commonly, they measure themselves by their inferiors, and because there are people several degrees below them morally they reckon themselves saints. "Well, I guess I am not the worst in town, by a long shot," men will say, as though that were much to their credit. All this sadly lowers a man's power of true self-estimate. What ought to be the standard by which we judge of our actions?

For this reason men need to keep Christ's example continually before them. No one can truly measure himself by Jesus' life and spirit and retain any pride. Our supposed superiorities dwindle when set alongside his towering greatness. Then we see our own limitations, feel our own need of merciful judgment, and go out from his presence, ready to be more forgiving to those who have offended us, more kindly and sympathetic in our estimates and judgments. "Be ye kind one to another, tenderhearted, forgiving each other, even as God also in Christ forgave you" (Eph. 4. 32). Not the smallest part of this influence is Jesus' own example of the merciful, magnanimous spirit. He loved his enemies, did good to those who hated him, blessed those that cursed him, and prayed for those who despitefully used him, even on the cross praying for his murderers, "Father, forgive them; for they know not what they do."

THE EVERYDAY PROBLEM

Daily life makes large drains on the forgiving spirit. Think over the injuries done to you which you find it hard to forgive. Sometimes it is financial offenses that are most felt, the competitor who takes away trade, or whose business grows faster than ours, or who causes us loss. Sometimes, strange to say, the bitterest resentment is felt by men against those who differ from them on some political or religious question. Others feel most an injury to pride, some disparagement or patronage or slight. What offenses do you find it hardest to forgive? No matter of what sort the injury is, this parable gives us a simple rule for dealing with it: take the most grievous injury and the one hardest to forgive and measure it with your own need of forgiveness from God.

A LAW OF THE KINGDOM

By its very nature, a merciful disposition is a unifying force. It reduces the harsh points of separation between people, between classes, between nations. It is absolutely essential to the Kingdom. If society is to be held together in peace and good will, no outer force of law or police can do it. It must be held together by the inward disposition of each member of it to forgive and be on terms of brotherly kindness with every other member.

As illustrations of the necessity of this law in national affairs consider the problems of establishing world peace and industrial peace. To reach peaceful and just relations between nation and nation, the spirit of revenge and of cherishing old grudges must be overcome and put away. No peace between nation and nation is secure when one harbors against the other a feeling of unforgiving animosity for injuries done or cherishes a desire for retaliation. When that hard spirit of ill will controls, the most elaborate peace treaties are in reality mere "scraps of paper." The Christian spirit of forgiveness, of mutual forbearance, of charitable and fair judgment is the only secure foundation for peace. The same is true of industrial peace. As long as employer and employee stand arrayed against each other, each cherishing the remembrance of the wrong the other has done to him, the possibility of that animosity breaking out into open conflict is held open. The only way in which both can advance to a working harmony that shall bring about justice to all is by overcoming the spirit of ill will. Both must let the determining consideration in all questions be, not the wrongs of the past, but the rights of all in the present day and the largest good of all in the future. For such tasks there is no adequate force on earth but the gospel of the love of God in Christ.

FOR REFLECTION AND DISCUSSION

How does Christian forgiveness differ from mere indifference to offenses against us? How from fear of protest? What is the moral effect of our indifference or fear on the offender?

Can a person really pray and at the same time cherish bitterness? Can you hate a man after sincerely praying for him? Have you ever tried praying for your enemies?

What offenses do you find it hardest to forgive? Is there any offense too great to be forgiven?

What is the application of this parable to our estimate and treatment of the immigrant in the United States? What is its application to our treatment of the criminal and prison reform?

What effect does carrying a "grudge" against another person have? Can you describe its effect from experience?

What effect has Christianity had on revenge, feuds, retaliation?

What is the attitude we should take toward those offenders who neither ask nor desire our forgiveness? Does Jesus' example throw any light on this question? For instance, his words on the cross?

CHAPTER IX

THE TALENTS

Matthew 25. 14-30

"For the case is that of a man going abroad, who summoned his servants and handed over his property to them; to one he gave twelve hundred pounds, to another five hundred, and to another two hundred and fifty; each got according to his capacity. Then the man went abroad. The servant who had got the twelve hundred pounds at once went and traded with them, making another twelve hundred. Similarly the servant who had got the five hundred pounds made another five hundred. But the servant who had got the two hundred and fifty pounds went off and dug a hole in the ground and hid his master's money. Now a long time afterwards the master of those servants came back and settled accounts with them. Then the servant who had got the twelve hundred pounds came forward, bringing twelve hundred more; he said, 'You handed me twelve hundred pounds, sir; here I have gained another twelve hundred.' His master said to him, 'Capital, you excellent and trusty servant! You have been trusty in charge of a small sum: I will put you in charge of a large sum. Come and share your master's feast.' Then the servant with the five hundred pounds came forward. He said, 'You handed me five hundred pounds, sir; here I have gained another five hundred.' His master said to him, 'Capital, you excellent and trusty servant! You have been trusty in charge of a small sum: I will put you in charge of a large sum. Come and share your master's feast.' Then the servant who had got the two hundred and fifty pounds came forward. He said, 'I knew you were a hard man, sir, reaping where you never sowed and gathering where you never winnowed. So I was afraid; I went and hid your two hundred and fifty pounds in the earth. There's your money!' His master said to him in reply, 'You rascal, you idle servant! You knew, did you, that I reap where I have never sowed and gather where I have never winnowed! Well then, you should have handed my money to the bankers and I would have got my capital with interest when I came back. Take therefore the two hundred and fifty pounds away from him, give it to the servant who had the twelve hundred.

For to everyone who has shall more be given and richly
    given;
but from him who has nothing, even what he has shall
    be taken.
Throw the good-for-nothing servant into the darkness outside; there men will wail and gnash their teeth."

THE TRAGEDY OF SLOTH

WHEN we confront such a vivid portrayal of human life
as we find in the Parable of the Talents, we can well appreciate two words of Scripture about Jesus:—"He knew
what was in man"; "never man so spake." Serious and
thought-provoking as it must have been on the solemn day
when it first came from Jesus' lips, it is just as arresting
and searching a warning to-day. For it deals with one of
the most insistent problems of life—with energy and faithfulness in the use of our abilities; with plain everyday
fidelity to duty. It deals with it both on the positive
and negative side. It portrays the splendor and high reward of Christian energy. It pictures also the tragedy of
sloth.

The warning sounded in the Parable of the Virgins is
against negligence. Here it is against indolence. They
are both perils to the religious life and to the Kingdom, but
they are perils of a different kind. Trench suggests that
the Parable of the Virgins shows the dangers of thoughtless overconfidence; that of the Talents shows the danger
of underconfidence and paralyzing fear. "The virgins
counted it too easy a thing to serve the Lord. The man
with one talent counted it too hard."

THE SPLENDOR OF CHRISTIAN ENERGY

In the strongest possible way Jesus in this parable commends and applauds the virtue of energy in the kingdom
of God. Indeed, in this we have an instance, in striking
form, of an interest and emphasis which runs all through
the parables. A recent writer[1] has pointed out how many

----

[1] T. R. Glover, The Jesus of History, p. 130.

of the parables turn on energy, showing how intensely
Jesus admired energy, and decision, and what a high place
he gave to them in his valuation of human qualities. "These
are the things that Jesus admires—in the widow who *will*
have justice (Luke 18. 2) ; in the virgins who thought
ahead and bought extra oil (Matt. 25. 4) ; in the vigorous
man who found the treasure and made sure of it (Matt. 13.
44) ; in the friend at midnight, who hammered, hammered,
hammered, till he got his loaves (Luke 11. 8). Even the bad
steward he commends because he definitely put his mind on
his situation (Luke 16. 8)." How does this emphasis of
Jesus on the high value and need of energetic action correspond to your experience? From which cause does the
usefulness of men suffer more, ignorance of what is needed
or lack of will and energy to work for it? We are fond of
singing, "Like a mighty army moves the Church of God."
But does it? In some places it moves more like a formal procession, a Memorial Day parade perhaps. Or, if it is an
army, its members stand like a company of soldiers which
has received the command, "At ease!" with all their guns
at "parade rest." Think of the various tasks of the Kingdom in your community, all the movements and associa-
tions for civic and moral and religious welfare. Which
retards their work and progress more, the opposition of
their opponents or the languid indifference of their
"friends"? Study the parable with the idea of finding the
cause and cure of this arch enemy of the Kingdom.

A CROSS SECTION OF LIFE

The parable is a true picture of life in its representation
of the master leaving with his three servants three different
amounts ranging from one talent (of the value of about
twelve hundred dollars) up to ten talents. In no other
way could a world where people vary so greatly in native
endowment, wealth, training, opportunity be fairly represented. If we look only at the inequalities of distribution
of natural capacity, environment, and opportunity, it seems
to be unjust. The truth which Jesus makes clear here must
always be remembered in connection with the unequal
division of ability and means. In God's sight a man's

character and his real achievement in life are determined by the fidelity and energy with which he has used the abilities with which he is endowed. The servant who gained ten pounds did not receive a whit more honor or reward than the one who had gained five. Each received the same eager and hearty "Well done, good and faithful servant!"

"All service ranks the same with God. There is no first or last." He judges by our unseen loyalties and fidelities. This is a commonplace to one familiar with Jesus' teaching. But it is one of those commonplaces which, if we only believed them, would change the face of the world overnight. A vast amount of somnolent self-satisfaction would speedily disappear if men earnestly believed that they would be judged in exact proportion to their use of their abilities and means. Two men may be about alike as far as their actual deeds are concerned. But one may be coming up from ignorance and coarse surroundings to a higher level of living, while the other is slipping down from the advantages of education and culture to a level of brutal dissipation. To the outward eye they seem to be just alike. In reality, in God's sight, the one slipping down is far more blameworthy than the other. Remember Jesus' words to the startled Pharisees who had had high spiritual privilege: "The publicans and the harlots go into the kingdom of God before you." Think of the advantages of birth, surroundings, friends, education, spiritual influences which are among the "talents" given you, and which must be weighed in determining your worth or slackness. Are men accustomed to overestimate or underestimate their advantages? their abilities? Why?

THE SLACKER WHO HID HIS TALENT

The main point of the parable, of course, has to do with the man who brought no gain to his Lord on his return. It is his failure and his fate which carry the warning to us. More nearly than either of the other two servants, his situation corresponds to that of the great majority of us, with our small amounts of ability and wealth.

It is no accident that the man who buried his talent was

the servant who had only one and not the one who had five or ten. The temptation to bury our abilities and fail to use them energetically comes with peculiar force to those of us who have only an ordinary amount. The man who is richly endowed in ability or wealth has his own keen temptations. He has the temptation to be wasteful or selfish. But he does not have the temptation of not using his powers at all.

The parable fairly shouts its warning to the man who hides his talent from use. Notice that it is not the man who "wastes his substance in riotous living" who is under condemnation here. The spending of wealth, of physical strength, and of the finer possibilities in coarse physical dissipation is a sin with a tragedy peculiar to itself. But that is not the kind of sin this unprofitable servant represents. There is no suggestion that he spent a penny of his lord's wealth on pleasure for himself; no hint that in any way he was given to coarse indulgence. He was quite respectable. He simply failed to use his talent for his master's benefit. But that failure was enough to cast him into outer darkness.

This message comes to those who, being equipped for activity, yet hide from active service; to the man who has no time to serve on committees; to the business man who will not give the value of his business ability to the church or charity; to the suburbanite who answers every request for service with an irritated, "I moved out here to rest"; to the college graduate who will give no effort to the higher life of the community; to the woman of experience who might be a force in the life of young girls, but who "can't be bothered"; to the man whose answer to appeals for concrete service in the church is "I have no talent for that sort of thing"; to the large and inglorious company of shirkers whom no man can number. How much Jesus' work in his life time was retarded by such merely negative goodness! How much the Kingdom is held back to-day by it! Think of the man who is an abstainer from liquor, but who will do nothing to fight the liquor traffic; who is pure in his own home life, but will not exert himself to clean up conditions which are an immoral influence in the town; who is himself a Christian believer, but who will not take off his coat and roll up his sleeves in an effort to extend Christianity in his own neighborhood. Are such people any different from the man who dug a hole in the ground and buried his talent there?

"I WAS AFRAID—"

In these words of excuse the man who hid his talent, gives voice to the chief reason for the waste of ability and means and the resulting feebleness and uselessness of multitudes of lives. It is frequently a miserable fear of mediocrity. People dislike to undertake tasks in which they can have only ordinary success or in which their performance will not be startling or brilliant. Their excuse is that they have no ability of any kind. It is worth noting that the parable does not recognize people without talent or ability. "God Almighty has no time to make nobodies," Spurgeon is reported to have said to one who sought to evade some proffered task on the ground that he was nobody! Yet how many make substantially the same excuse that they can do nothing, when what they truly mean is that they *will* do nothing, because their abilities are not of a dazzling order. The Master needs people who will sacrifice this childish pride to him and his cause, and repeat from their hearts the old, old formula of Edward Everett Hale: "I am only one, but I *am* one. I cannot do everything, but I *can* do something. And I will not let what I cannot do interfere with what I can do." Which represents your usual attitude to requests for service and help, these words of Dr. Hale's or the common reply, "O, no! I couldn't possibly do it. I'm no good at that sort of thing"?

We are morbidly afraid of mistakes. And that cowardly fear of a blunder or appearing a little awkward has kept thousands of men from doing a world of good while making a few mistakes. The ability of most men for public prayer or public witnessing for Christ is not large. They are afraid of saying the wrong thing, and as a result they say nothing and the cause of Christ, which would have gained immensely by the simple sincere word, suffers irreparable damage. Is this not a parallel case to the man who buried his talent in the ground? Remember, "the man who never made any mistakes never made anything else."

THE TYRANNY OF PETTY PRIDE

Pride is the real root of the trouble. Both forms of fear mentioned above, having the outward appearance of humility, are forms of pride. "As long as I haven't been given five talents, but have been put off with a miserable little one, I won't do anything with it." The man with one talent showed plainly in the excuses he offered just what was the matter with him. He had been thinking of himself all the time. Study that excuse of his. He never gets his eye off himself for a moment. It is his own justification, his own safety, which has occupied him, never the profit he desired to make for his master. The only cure for this paralyzing self-consciousness is to learn to care about those we can help. If we really love and truly want to help, we will not stop to ask whether we are getting enough publicity or whether some one else is doing more than we. Think of the tremendous energies which could be let loose for the kingdom of God if people could only forego the gratification of their little pride of reputation and throw themselves into the nearest task that pleads for their help! While you are thinking of this vast amount of energy consider this also. Is any of it locked up in you? Is there anything which you are not doing because it does not seem particularly important or honorable, or because you cannot do it in a brilliant manner?

Jealousy of others has much to do with making slackers. No doubt this entered into the action of the man with one talent in the parable. Many think to show their qualification for the position of one above them by neglecting the one they have. Jealousy is another form of the same blighting pride. Too often the work and usefulness of a local church is halted by the jealous pride of some who, like Cæsar, would rather be first in some little Alpine village than second or third in Rome. They will serve as long as they are directing. They are quite willing to be brigadier-generals in the army of the Lord but cannot bring

themselves to enlist as a private. How may envy and
jealousy of another's superior ability or position be overcome?

"If Things Were Only Different"

Perhaps the commonest form of burying our talent is
idly and uselessly to think and talk about what we would
do if we were in other conditions or had larger opportunities, doing nothing meanwhile with the conditions and
opportunities we actually have. It is a cheap and popular
way of excusing an inexcusable indolence. All who make
such futile excuses are lineal descendants of the man who
hid his lord's money. One man will bewail his lack of
wealth and imagine how much he would do if he only had
two thousand dollars instead of one. Another will say that
if he only had great abilities he would achieve great things.
Another is convinced that if he had a more important position instead of the obscure place he occupies, or were in
a more congenial place rather than among the stupid and
unresponsive people with whom he lives, he would render
distinguished service. All such imaginings are a delusion
and a drug to the conscience. They overlook two important truths: that a man's real achievement is measured
by the use made of what he has, be it large or small; and
that the only sure indication of what one would do with
larger means or talents is what he actually does do with
the smaller ones which are his.

The Penalty of Disuse

When the parable represents the talent as taken away
from the man who did not use it, it pictures a law which
holds sway in the physical, economic, and intellectual world
as well as the spiritual. That the faculty which we do
not invest in active service will be taken from us is a
"natural law in the spiritual world." The arm which is
never exercised loses its strength by degrees as muscles
and sinews shrink. When we arise from a sickness of only
a few weeks we have to learn to walk all over again. In
that short time the deadening process has gone so far that
our limbs are unable to support us. The man who does

not use his mind, soon has none to use, and must eke out
a miserable intellectual existence by borrowing catchwords
from his neighbors. The business man who does not constantly get new business soon files a petition in bankruptcy.
So the powers which God has given us fail if we do not
exercise them. Nothing can be sadder than to watch this
law operate in some friend's life. The capacity for enthusiasm, the appetite for spiritual things, the ability to
see visions, the energy of toil, the unselfish spirit of sacrifice—all these, the finest flowers of earth, wither and droop,
where they are not brought to fruitage for the Lord of the
vineyard. Perhaps we sacrifice our powers on the altar
of the pagan gods of financial success, comfortable ease,
or sodden pleasure. Whether our lives shall be this sordid
dwindling of power or an increase in usefulness and joy
which "groweth more and more even unto the perfect day"
is being surely determined by the use we are now making
of everything we have.

For Reflection and Discussion

What influence does a wrong idea of God have on our conduct? How is this illustrated by the man with one
talent?

What is the reward of the servants who had five and two
talents? What are the rewards of energetic Christian
activity?

What teachings of Jesus bear on the problem of overcoming envy and jealousy? What other parts of the Bible
bear on the same problems?

Is the common idea of Jesus always that of a man of
energy? If it is not, why not? What indications can
you give that he was a man of energy?

Put this parable into terms of life—describe three business
men in your own town, three farmers, or three house-
wives, who correspond to the three servants.

What has been your own experience of the law of disuse?
Has your own prayer increased or decreased? Your
readiness of response to need? your willingness to incur
unpopularity?

Where does the church receive the majority of its support, from the five-talented rich or the people of one talent? Is there any talent which cannot be used in the church?

What has been the effect of Christianity on idleness? Do Christian people really believe that uselessness is immoral?

How did Jesus oppose the idea of God as a severe taskmaster? See Matthew 23. 23; Luke 18. 12; Mark 7. 34.

Should a Christian "go into politics"?

CHAPTER X

THE PHARISEE AND THE PUBLICAN

Luke 18. 9-14

He also told the following parable to certain persons who were sure of their own goodness and looked down upon everybody else. "Two men went up to pray in the temple; one was a Pharisee and the other was a taxgatherer. The Pharisee stood up and prayed by himself as follows: 'I thank thee, O God, I am not like the rest of men, thieves, rogues, and immoral, or even like yon taxgatherer. Twice a week I fast; on all my income I pay tithes.' But the taxgatherer stood far away and would not lift even his eyes to heaven, but beat his breast, saying, 'O God, have mercy on me for my sins!' I tell you, he went home accepted by God rather than the other man;

for everyone who uplifts himself will be humbled,
  and he who humbles himself will be uplifted."

AN ACID TEST OF CHARACTER

THERE is very little about a man—actions, manner, or even physical characteristics—which does not reveal character. Speech, likes and dislikes, gestures, expressions, and habits are all sure indicators of character to the keen observer. But nothing reveals the real man with quite so bright a glare as his private prayers. What he actually is is surely revealed when he prays. The strength or feebleness of a man's soul, its glow of health or blight of disease, stands out unmistakably then. The strongest way in which Jesus could reveal the contrasted character of the Pharisee and publican was to show them at prayer. The parable is more than a parable on the nature of prayer. It is a vivid study of the characters of which the prayers are an indication. It is a red light of warning against the pitfalls of hard and unsympathetic pride. It is a tender plea for those

fragrant qualities of character which are the very soul of
the kingdom of God and without which none can enter it
—humility, penitence, meekness, and hunger and thirst
after righteousness.

"Two men went up into the temple to pray; the one a
Pharisee, and the other a publican." They went up in
Jesus' day. They went up to church last Sunday. They
will be there again next Sunday. They live on our block.
They walk our streets. They come into our houses. We
see them everywhere we turn, even when we look in the
mirror. Let us study what meaning they may have for us;
how they came to be what they were; and, above all, let
us discover how it was that, with so many good deeds to
his credit, the Pharisee was nevertheless a thing odious to
God and man; while the publican, with so much evil-doing
against him, found his way into the pathway of blessing
and grace.

THE CONTRAST

Tennyson speaks of "the fierce light that beats about a
throne." There is an even fiercer light that beats about the
altar of prayer, and as these men go up to pray it reveals
their inmost being, as by a very X-ray, to the One "to whom
all hearts are open, all desires known, and from whom no
secrets are hid." Jesus brings out the contrast between
them in swift and telling strokes. There was a contrast in
very attitude. The Pharisee "stood and prayed" confidently
and conspicuously; the publican, at a distance, lowers his
eyes to the ground in shame. There is a mute eloquence
in the bodily posture that speaks of pride or humility. The
posture represents a contrast in spirit; the Pharisee, self
satisfied—"I thank thee, that I am not as the rest of men";
the publican, "poor in spirit"—"me a sinner." There is
a glaring contrast in the prayer itself. The Pharisee asks
nothing, simply delivers himself of a self-centered imperti-
nent soliloquy—"I fast," "I give tithes." The publican
calls out of a crushing need. There is a difference of object.
The publican prays to God; the Pharisee, while he mentions God respectfully, gives his attention mainly to himself and to his neighbors. And, of course, the climax of

it all is a contrast in result: the Pharisee, not heard of God, unchanged in any way; the publican, "justified."

THE MAN WHO PRAYED WITH HIMSELF

Let us listen more closely to this monologue which the Pharisee holds with himself. It can teach us much.

With a keen thrust of irony Jesus indicated the fatal flaw in the Pharisee's prayer when he said that he prayed with *himself*. The description reminds us somewhat of the prayer which has gone down in history as "the most eloquent prayer ever addressed to a Boston audience." The Pharisee's prayer was not addressed to God but to a Jerusalem audience composed of himself. In the opening thanksgiving God seems to be mentioned in a complimentary remark, but we soon discover that the subject and object of his prayer are the same, himself. We can hear the "I, I, I," go thumping all the way through his address like a flat wheel on a trolley car.

It was not prayer because he felt no need. The essence of prayer is desire. It expresses a need and voices a want. How ridiculous it would be to call the Pharisee's self-congratulation "asking," "seeking," or "knocking," the words which Jesus used to describe prayer!

> "Prayer is the soul's sincere desire,
> Uttered or unexpressed;
> The motion of a hidden fire
> That trembles in the breast."

Notice how well the agonizing petition of the publican, "God, be thou merciful to me a sinner," fulfils that description of prayer.

> "Two men went up to pray? Oh, rather say,
> One went to brag, the other went to pray."

Self-satisfied pride can never pray. It is the climax of the spiritual blight which pride inflicts, that it stifles the sense of need out of which all true prayer, communion with God, is born.

The Pharisee's prayer was unneighborly, and so impossible as a prayer, for all true prayer is neighborly in feeling.

The word "Pharisee" means "Separatist" and this particular one more than lived up to the name. No "separatist" who, in his thinking, holds himself aloof from others can pray in the Christian sense. The grim and certain penalty of separating ourselves from our fellow men is that we separate ourselves from God. Can you imagine the Pharisee standing with the publican and saying, "Our Father . . . forgive us our trespasses and give us this day our daily bread"? Yet no other kind of prayer is acceptable. Have you clearly realized that? Have you thought what it means that in the Lord's Prayer one is bound by the very words of the prayer to join himself in thought and sympathy with his fellow men?

This unsocial quality of the Pharisee's prayer appears in its censoriousness. When a man truly prays he has no time to gaze around at his neighbor's faults. The earnestness of his own need preoccupies him. It is significant that, even though he was praying, the Pharisee let his eye travel around the room till it caught sight of the publican and promptly seized upon him as an example of sin. "A man never comes near to God when his mind is wandering hither and thither in censorious criticism of his fellow men. In prayer we look up in aspiration or we look down in humility; we never look around in criticism or curiosity" (Hubbard). This hard, censorious habit of the Pharisee fed his self-esteem and self-satisfaction. Can you tell from experience how rapidly a censorious and critical habit grows? Note its effect on the Pharisee. Most other people are to him "extortioners, unjust, adulterers." This poor publican, whom he had doubtless never seen before, he quickly assumes to be bad. What effect does a fault-finding disposition have on one's spiritual life? One's own power of enjoyment? How may it be overcome?

Through the clear window of his prayer we discover a distortion. He has a wrong idea of *goodness* as a thing of negative abstinences and outward acts. He has a false idea of *religion* as ceremony and no conception of it as "the life of God in the soul of man." He has no idea of the relation between the two, his religion having no result in positive morality, such as love, service or humility.

The Pharisee We Know Best

The Pharisee of A. D. 31 is interesting and important chiefly for the light he throws on the Pharisee of A. D. Nineteen Hundred and To-day. Across the centuries there sounds the warning which Jesus first gave to his disciples, as, crowded together in a little boat one night, they sailed across the Galilæan lake: "Beware of the leaven of the Pharisees."

Back of all the Pharisee's blunders in religion and character is mistaking the means for the end. Prayers, ceremonies, worship are useful only as a means of bringing men into communion with God, making them like God in character, and developing a love for God and their fellow men. When observances and worship have no results in character and service they are useless. We are guilty of the sin of the Pharisee when our worship brings forth no fruit in our lives or when we allow the outward observances of religion to take first place in importance over the great plain matters of right conduct, of sympathy and love, and of that humble, childlike attitude of spirit, without which no man enters the Kingdom.

When the question is asked whether a person is religious or not, what kinds of facts are mentioned as evidence, facts of conduct and inner disposition or facts of observance of well-established religious customs? The process by which a Pharisee is made is a subtle and unconscious one beginning with false standards of worth. It is ever so much easier to go to church every Sunday, or to say our prayers every day, than to keep ourselves from slandering or from impure thought, from losing our temper, or to refrain from envy, from selfishness and coldness. We substitute the lower standard for the higher. We fulfil the outward, mechanical standard and thereby become self-satisfied. We may lose the hunger and thirst after real inner righteousness and another Pharisee is made.

A Look in the Mirror

We need a continual guard lest we become *intellectual pharisees*. Early opportunities of education and environ-

ment have undeniably set us above many of our fellows.
What effect have these advantages had on us? Have they
made us snobbish, distant, superior? If so, it is a question whether they ought to be called advantages, for expansion of the mind is a poor compensation for contrac-
tion of the heart. Do we ever feel thankful that we are
not like the crude, loud, ignorant family across the street
or "the masses" on the other side of town? There is a
pernicious habit of affecting to be bored by the common
and simpler pleasures in which the great majority find
joy. People who have that habit, in most cases educated
people, seem to feel that to join in the common emotions
of the multitude is an evidence of inferiority. They only
prove that "a little learning is a dangerous thing." Education is a responsibility, a trust which we are charged to
administer for the benefit of others. It is not an empty
decoration to be worn with exultation.

Racial pharisees obstruct the coming of the kingdom of
God. Men of the Anglo-Saxon race with little or no understanding or appreciation of the genius and virtues of
Oriental races, frequently look upon them with contempt.
Men of every race are too prone to regard every difference
from themselves as a defect, when in truth it may be a
vast superiority. The only way in which thousands of
Americans ever treat the immigrants from Russia and
southeastern Europe is with a superior contempt or patronage. Yet thousands of these immigrants have displayed
a heroic devotion to liberty, a capacity for unselfish sacrifice, and an endless industry far beyond anything to which
the Americans who looked down upon them could aspire.
Have you ever known any examples of this? How may
this narrow-minded provincialism be overcome?

Social pharisaism is quite as vicious in its effects. Differences of wealth, of occupation, of position, too often
cause an attitude even in Christian people, which cannot
be distinguished from the Pharisee's miserable boast, "God,
I thank thee, that I am not as the rest of men." Vast
numbers of people are "separatists," so far as any real
contact with people who have to work for a living is concerned. Every city has its social clique whose members

regard themselves as a veritable Brahman caste. Sometimes that ugly spirit of class distinction does not even stop at the door of the Christian church, but enters in to profane the sanctuary by its crass denial of the message of Jesus.

The sectarian pharisee effectually blocks the deep desire of Christ "that they may all be one." Happily, his tribe is decreasing. The church in all sections has had marvelous growth in recent years in the capacity for generous enthusiasm and appreciation for the excellences of other denominations. But the pharisaic spirit of "holier than thou" has kept different bodies far apart. Alexander Whyte says truly, "It is not so much our love of truth which has kept us apart as our love of ourselves."

Have you ever thought of the serious implications in the fact that Jesus said of the Pharisees, "Let them alone"? He was the most undiscourageable optimist who ever walked the earth. He saw the good possibilities in the greatest sinners. Yet he regarded this self-satisfied, hard formalism of the Pharisees as the most hopeless thing in the world.

THE PRAYER THAT GOD HEARD

The sincerity of the publican's prayer shines out in the directness and intensity of his plea. "When the heart is stirred it speaks in telegrams." As we hear him pray, the Beatitudes come to mind. He embodies perfectly the basic qualities which Jesus calls blessed, and so is a perfect model on which to form our prayers. "Blessed are the poor in spirit." "Blessed are they that mourn. Blessed are the meek." "Blessed are they that hunger and thirst after righteousness." These qualities in one's life are open doors through which God enters, bearing the gifts of pardon and power. A hard, erect impenitence is like a stone wall around one's life effectually shutting out all possibility of forgiveness. The priceless worth of a penitent spirit is beautifully expressed in Moore's "Paradise and the Peri," in Lalla Rookh, in which a Peri was refused admission to paradise until she brought the most precious thing on earth. She tried in vain with the last drop of a patriot's life blood and the last sigh of a lover's self-sacrifice, but finally was admitted when she bore up to the gate a tear of penitence of an old man. There is a sure spiritual insight in the story, for, according to Jesus, penitence is the most precious thing on earth.

Consider how humility of spirit and a sense of sinfulness have been a mark of the greatest characters in Christian history. Remember Paul's "Christ Jesus came into the world to save sinners; of whom I am chief," and Luther's last words, written on a piece of paper, "We are all beggars, that is true." The more one knows of God, the keener sensitiveness he has for his own sin. True spiritual progress will always be marked by the spirit of penitence shown in the publican's prayer.

"What Shall I Do to be Saved?"

How shall we be saved from the infection of formalism, of pride, of hardness? How shall we keep alive the spirit of humility and sympathy? It is every man's own battle and he must win it by his own strategy. But there are certain great aids which are available for all. First, much is gained when we recognize that it is a battle and our most important one. The weakening of the inner life of the spirit comes through carelessness and neglect. Second, we preserve a true estimate of ourselves by constantly taking Christ as a model and aspiring to be like him. There is no room for petty self-satisfaction or congratulatory comparison with others, when beside the strength and goodness of Jesus our best achievement seems but a poor blunder. The little hills around our homes seem high until we see the Rockies or the Alps; so our petty superiorities melt away as we come to know Jesus. When that knowledge is burned into our hearts there is only one prayer that rises to our lips—"God, be merciful to me a sinner!" Third, constant sympathetic contact with others and service with and for them saves us from selfishness. It lifts us out of the narrow provinciality that so easily besets us. It delivers us from getting into the condition of those for whose express benefit Jesus told this story—"who trusted in themselves that they were righteous, and set all others at nought." When we work with people and really know them, we learn to appreciate them. It is contact with the native water carrier of India on the firing line which wrings from Tommy Atkins the admission that Gunga Din is a better man than himself.

FOR REFLECTION AND DISCUSSION

What light do the Beatitudes throw on prayer? How far can a man's character be measured by prayer?

Read the descriptions of Pharisees in the following references: Matthew 5. 20; 6. 1-8; 23. 1-35; Mark 7. 1-13; John 7. 45-49. What characteristics are shown? Did the Pharisees have any good qualities? What were they?

Compare the publican's prayer with some of the "model" prayers of Paul: Philippians 3. 7-14 and 1 Corinthians 2. 9. What have they in common? How much social feeling do you have in prayer?

What place had prayer in Jesus' own life? When did he pray? What were the results?

Is there a pharisaism of education? Of class? Of nation?

What means of religious education may be used to develop the sense of brotherhood and humility?

Is a sense of unworthiness an indication of strength or weakness of character? What is the difference between the spirit of Pharisees and self-reliance?

What are class lines drawn in your town? What are their effects?

What experience have we had of refusal to associate with others? For what reason did we refuse, on account of wealth, education, race, or religion?

CHAPTER XI

THE RICH FOOL

Luke 12. 13-21

A man out of the crowd said to him, "Teacher, tell my brother to give me my share of our inheritance"; but he said to him, "Man, who made me a judge or arbitrator over your affairs?" Then he said to them, "See and keep clear of covetousness in every shape and form, for a man's life is not part of his possessions because he has ample wealth." And he told them a parable. "A rich man's estate bore heavy crops. So he debated, 'What am I to do? I have no room to store my crops.' And he said, 'This is what I will do. I will pull down my granaries and build larger ones, where I can store all my produce and my goods. And I will say to my soul, "Soul, you have ample stores laid up for many a year; take your ease, eat, drink and be merry."' But God said to him, 'Foolish man, this very night your soul is wanted; and who will get all you have prepared?' So fares the man who lays up treasure for himself instead of gaining the riches of God."

A LIFE OR A LIVING?

It was Governor William E. Russell, of Massachusetts, who, about a generation ago, set afloat on the stream of American thought and speech the striking and fruitful sentence, "It is better to make a life than a living." That clear and fine distinction expresses much of Jesus' teaching about wealth, its use and its perils. In particular it emphasizes the meaning of the Parable of the Rich Fool, for the bitter and stupid tragedy of that prosperous farmer lay in allowing the secondary and minor business of making and spending a living to crowd out the sublime business of making a life and growing a soul.

It is a parable for busy, active, and successful people. In many ways it seems peculiarly an American parable. There is in America an abundant production of raw material, an unparalleled agricultural and industrial development, coupled with an amazing genius for invention and manipulation which is at once a glory and a peril. The man had many qualities which we are accustomed to think of and applaud as typically American. He was energetic and efficient. His fields bore "bumper" crops. He was a man of foresight, and of decision, "This will I do." He would have made an excellent manager of a growing department store or a manufacturing plant. Yet in spite of these interesting qualities Jesus called him a fool. Surely, here is something which demands of us in the midst of our busy, pushing American life of growing prosperity, that we "Stop, Look, and Listen."

AN INTERRUPTED ADDRESS

Suppose that as Abraham Lincoln was finishing his Second Inaugural Address and had just reached the lofty paragraph beginning "With malice toward none," some persistent office-seeker had interrupted him loudly demanding to be appointed to a position. Or suppose that some one should interrupt an impressive sermon to a large congregation by clamoring for the ushers to show him to a better seat. With such situations in mind we realize the untimeliness of the man who interrupted Jesus to demand his brother be made to share the inheritance with him. It was a discourse of rare beauty on trust, and Jesus had just assured his disciples of the sure presence of God's spirit with them. But it did not take this man's mind from his own grievance. He felt himself defrauded and disinherited. Perhaps he was a younger brother who was disgruntled because the elder brother had the double portion allotted to him by law (Deut. 21. 17). At all events, he has so far lost his sense of the relative values and importance of things, his own affairs are so all important, that, as he listens to the matchless speaker, all he can think of is how he can use him for his own financial gain.

While it was easy to interrupt Jesus, it was impossible for anyone to throw him off the track or entangle him. Refusing to pronounce on the justice of the claim, or even to listen to it, he passes swiftly to point out the deeper evil from which the man is suffering, covetousness. "Keep yourselves from all covetousness," he pleads, "for a man's life consisteth not in the abundance of things which he possesseth." He enforces the plea with a story which convincingly portrays the supreme folly into which covetousness brings men, the Parable of the Rich Fool.

JESUS AND THE STATE

The incident which gave rise to this parable is more than ordinarily instructive and valuable. It shows Jesus definitely and positively refusing to pronounce on a matter which belonged to the courts and the law of the land. He will not enter into the realm of making legal and economic and political regulations, though men try desperately to get him to do so. At the same time he does pronounce unsparingly and unmistakably on the spiritual issues underlying the question. He does not come among men as a new judge and divider or as the maker of a new code of criminal law. But he does come to seek and to save those who are lost in the clutches of covetousness and greed. It is just because he brought spiritual truth to men and refused to let that spiritual truth be abandoned in favor of some local and ephemeral economic and political scheme, that his words do not pass away. Had Jesus made a collection of laws which fitted the commercial and industrial life of Palestine in A. D. 30, they would have been unsuited to other countries and other centuries with far different conditions, and Christianity would have died with the kind of life to which it was adapted. But Jesus' words are "spirit and life." They give the principles, values and motives by which men can construct right government, laws, and social conditions. From the study of this action of Jesus it would seem that the church follows his example most closely when it proclaims the Christian principles which must control actions and the human and spiritual values which must be conserved in the state and in industry, rather than by identifying Christianity with any particular political or economic regime. We are often assured by socialists that "Christianity means socialism." The effort to identify Christianity with any particular form of social order is a modern form of the demand, "Speak to my brother that he divide the inheritance with me." Can Christianity be identified with any scheme of social reorganization? What is the relation between Christianity and various measures of social betterment?

THE TRAGEDY OF SUCCESS

A not uncommon form of fatal accident which happens in the great grain elevators is that of a man being buried under a mountain of wheat. It is a particularly striking form of tragedy. The wheat, a means of supporting life, becomes the instrument of destroying it. It was a similar tragedy which overtook this prosperous farmer, that of having his real life, the life of the spirit, buried and crushed out under an avalanche of produce. It was a tragedy of success, the blinding of the man to the real purpose and use of life by the mere accumulation of things. Its cause is the failure to recognize a higher life which does not depend on wealth. As Jesus used the word "life" it has two meanings, one the physical existence, depending on the acquisition of food, drink, clothing, and shelter. The other is a life of the spirit which depends on the acquisition of relationships, of ideals, of memories and emotions. This man says to his soul, "Soul, thou hast much goods laid up for many years," but there is irony in the language. What had he that a soul could live on? Can a man's soul, that spiritual self capable of an eternal fellowship with God, brotherhood with man, and aspiration to an ideal, live on vegetables? Can it thrive on wheat? Or on houses and lands? Is it any wonder, then, that Jesus called this man by that solemn name "fool"?

Instead of nourishing a life of the spirit this man's heart and mind had become a mere clutter of merchandise. That his soul had been flattened out by accumulated goods is clearly shown by two things. He did not recognize the source of his prosperity in God, from whom the increase came. Nor did he recognize the true purpose of his prosperity, ministry to others to whom the surplus should have gone. Blindness in these two directions shows that he has richly earned his title "fool." What littleness of soul a

man has who takes the bounty of nature with never a pause
to acknowledge the source, never a feeling of gratitude.
What a bankrupt heart he has when he can look at his
bursting barns and have no idea of sharing his abundance
with anyone! Says Rauschenbusch: "The man was a sub-
limated chipmunk, gloating over bushels of pignuts."
Whatever a man recognizes as the source of his wealth
largely determines the use to which he puts it.

> "Back of the loaf is the snowy flour,
>   And back of the flour, the mill;
> And back of the mill is the wheat and the shower,
>   The sun and the Father's will."

"No Pockets in a Shroud"

The grim Spanish proverb "There are no pockets in a
shroud" points out the other blunder made by this rich
fool and all the multitude of his imitators. He confused
himself with his possessions. His possessions seemed so
solid and real that he was blinded to the fact that they
were not a part of himself. There is no suggestion that he
was bad. He did not make his wealth dishonestly. Nor
is it implied that he spent it viciously. His invitation to
his soul, "Eat, drink, and be merry," does not contemplate
an immoral riot of sensuality so much as well fed comfort
and luxury. Jesus' warning is clear and simple. It is
against covetousness, the love of accumulation, not for the
sake of the good it will do, but for its own sake, a love of
accumulation so blind and strong that it crowds both God
and his fellow men out of a man's life.

Have you ever thought of how large a proportion of
Jesus' sayings have to do with the getting and spending of
wealth? Some one has estimated that it is nearly one half.
Did Jesus pay too much attention to it? Surely, if we
have observed how great a force in making character and
how severe a test of it the getting and spending of money
is, we speedily recognize that Jesus was right. If his
Kingdom is to survive and grow in the world, avarice and
covetousness must be conquered. Covetousness and Christian love can no more exist together than fire and water.

If a man is to become godlike in character, he must strangle covetousness in himself. Jesus' intense warning against covetousness is justified for two reasons. First, covetousness extends its blight over the whole of life. A great artist has given on canvas his conception of covetousness as having the forepart of the body like a dragon and the rear part like a shapeless iceberg. It is his portrayal of the truth that the approach of avarice freezes every fine enthusiasm and generous movement of the heart. Other vices spoil different aspects of life; this one chills it at the center. The other reason is that no vice is so hard to detect. There is a sharp warning in the statement of a priest that he had every conceivable sin on earth confessed to him except that of covetousness. It usually appears first under the guise of "thrift," "diligence," or "prudence," and is warmly welcomed. Then its coils tighten about the heart without our recognition and early ideals of unselfish service and sacrifice, our habits of generosity and capacity for enthusiasm are quietly strangled. It is hard to recognize the process. Anyone knows when he has been drunk, but who can tell when he is growing covetous?

ARE OUR STANDARDS OF LIFE CHRISTIAN?

Consider the standards of society to-day in the light of the place this man would occupy in your community. Remember that he is prosperous, diligent, and nowhere indicated as immoral. His chief purpose in life is accumulation of money, and he is selfish in the use of it. Would society strongly disapprove of him? It is useless to ask the question. He would be proudly referred to as "one of our substantial citizens." His erection of new additions to his buildings would be pointed to with pride. He would be made a director of half a dozen enterprises and his commonplace remarks gravely recorded in the newspaper. There is a strong possibility that he would even be elected a trustee of the church. Think of the meaning of these two facts: society honors a prosperous, progressive, and efficient man of this type; Jesus called him a fool. How far are our standards of judgment Christian? Are they becoming more Christian?

OWNERSHIP VERSUS STEWARDSHIP

The rich fool had a selfish theory of absolute ownership of the lands and produce which came into his possession, which always has selfish and sordid results in life. His life had none of the dignity and responsibility which the recognition of God and his providence can bring to any man. He had none of the joyous sense of partnership which a true conception of God gives. The Christian conception of life is based on the idea of stewardship. The true Christian does not think of holding property with a sense of absolute and irresponsible proprietorship, but with each privilege granted it hears the whisper of God— "Occupy till I come." He knows God as the giver of every good and perfect gift and counts it a high privilege to be a coworker with him in his plans of love. The steward-ship ideal of life is beautifully expressed in the Old Testament, "All things come of thee, and of thine own have we given thee. For we are strangers before thee, and sojourners, as all our fathers were: our days on earth are as a shadow." Such a feeling saves life from the curse of spending downward to the ruin of character and will lead it out into the grace and blessing of spending upward and making one's money serve the highest purposes.

THE NATION AS A FOOL

This story of the man who forgot the true end and purpose of life in the secondary business of providing the means has a direct application to social conditions. What shall it profit a nation, any more than a man, to gain the whole world and lose its own life? What shall it profit a nation if its vast wealth is piled up at the expense of the well-being of its workers? What benefit, after all, is the production of the finest steel on earth, if men are worn out, crippled, or degraded in the process? What is the value of all the cotton goods the country produces if the cost of its production is a stunted and weakened and de-frauded childhood? Grim old Thomas Carlyle cried, many years ago, when England was making this stupendous blunder of child labor, "If you have to take the devil into partnership in the cotton business, give up the cotton business!" Is a state or town wise in thinking that it profits by the money returns of its saloon licenses, when the real cost in degraded manhood is forgotten? States and communities which do any of these things are rich fools. *The true test of any system of industry is not the amount of goods it produces, but its effect upon men.* When the social order becomes Christianized that truth will be exalted to a ruling position.

"FIGHT THE GOOD FIGHT WITH ALL THY MIGHT!"

And surely it is a fight to which we are called. We must win our fight against covetousness in its very citadel, the market place. The very circumstances of our lives and occupations decree us to traffic in things, continually to gather produce, build barns, and sell in exchanges. How can we so do it that our barns and produce do not fall upon us and crush out the highest possibilities and powers of our lives?

It was to that very problem that Jesus addressed himself when he finished speaking this parable. Read Luke 12. 22-34 carefully for Jesus' practical directions for its solution. Notice the forces which he offers us, gratitude, trust, and prayer. Remember what a part these forces played in his own life. The surest way of overcoming the pressure from the material world on our spiritual life is by the stronger counter pressure of an inward spiritual life maintained at full strength.

FOR REFLECTION AND DISCUSSION

What were the aids which Jesus used in overcoming the temptation to found a materialistic kingdom. Matthew 4. 1-11; 16. 23.

How does the teaching of this parable compare with Jesus' other teaching about wealth? Compare Matthew 6. 24-34; Luke 9. 25; Mark 10. 23-31; Luke 6. 24. On the basis of these passages summarize Jesus' teaching about wealth.

Should the church "go into politics"? What should be the relation of the church to movements for social reform?

Compare the way in which a rich man who spends everything on himself is now regarded with the attitude of a generation ago? Has there been any growth in the feeling of the responsibilities of wealth? In what respects?

Would Jesus condemn a man who, having grown rich at the expense of the rights of others, gives his money generously to charity? How does Jesus' attitude toward wealth differ from the ordinary viewpoint of the modern world?

How would you spend a million dollars?

Do you know exactly how your income is spent? What proportion of it is spent for religious or charitable purposes? What would be a right proportion? Do God and money ever come into collision in your life?

What are the chief dangers of money-making? Why did Jesus talk so much about it? At what point does the amount of private wealth a man has become contrary to the principles of Jesus?

Is it in accordance with Christian principles to live without productive labor? Or to enjoy excessive leisure purchased by the excessive toil of others?

CHAPTER XII

THE MUSTARD SEED.   THE LEAVEN

Matthew 13. 31-33

He put another parable before them. "The Realm of heaven," he said, "is like a grain of mustard-seed which a man takes and sows in his field. It is less than any seed on earth, but when it grows up it is larger than any plant, it becomes a tree, so large that *the wild birds* come and *roost in its branches*."

He told them another parable. "The Realm of heaven," he said, "is like dough which a woman took and buried in three pecks of flour, till all of it was leavened."

Two Parables of Cheer

THE effect of the Parables of the Sower and the Tares must have been somewhat discouraging to the disciples. Both parables show with great and almost painful plainness the hindrances and difficulties in the way of the growth of the Kingdom. To realize that much of the seed will bring forth absolutely nothing and that much of evil must be allowed to remain alongside of the good, is certainly not enheartening. Thus it is no doubt part of the wise strategy of Jesus, that after two parables showing the obstacles and difficulties, he should give two parables which are magnificent stimulants to faith and energy. For they both declare that in spite of every barrier of opposition the kingdom of God is sure to extend on earth until it holds dominion everywhere and until it has infused its spirit into all society and transformed it with its leaven. Such a mighty and dominating faith as Jesus shows in these parables is surely the elixir of life to the church and to the individual disciple. Whenever men have shared in this calm, profound faith that God is to be victorious in

his world, it is to them a veritable draught from the fountain of youth. Under its influence they have mounted up
with wings as eagles; they have run and not been weary;
they have walked and not fainted.

The Need of Faith To-day

Would anyone say that a message of cheer and faith on
the sure growth and world-wide dominion of the kingdom
of God is uncalled for and unnecessary to-day? Is it not
far nearer the truth to say that the need of a reasoned
faith in the victory of God's kingdom in the world is one
of our deepest and most urgent needs? Was there ever
a time when the need for such faith was greater? Certainly, there was need that Jesus should speak these parables of reassurance to the disciples, as the beginning of
what was designed to be a conquest of the world seemed
so pitiably small and insignificant. They needed hearten-
ing and encouragement, and Jesus gave it to them. We do
not face the same strange, hostile Roman world that they
did. But we do look out on a world that is teeming with
depressing facts and alive with hostile forces. Only when
we shut our eyes can we deny them. The appalling losses
from war, losses physical, moral, and spiritual; the persis-
tence of ancient iniquities that debase and destroy; the injustices and wastes of industry; the inertia of ignorance
and indifference; the vast numbers and extent of the non-
Christian world—these are a few of the reasons why we
need supremely to catch the contagion of faith from Christ
and hear his voice repeating to our hearts, "The kingdom
of heaven is like unto a grain of mustard seed."

The Certainty of the Kingdom

The Parables of the Mustard Seed and of the Leaven
present differences of meaning which must be noted, but
their essential teaching is one. The comparison of the
Kingdom both to the mustard seed and to the leaven portrays the gradual but sure and increasing growth of the
kingdom of God until its dominion extends throughout the
world. This central truth is expressed in each parable
with a different emphasis. The tiny mustard seed growing

into a sizable tree represents the growth of the kingdom of God as a visible society which can be seen or numbered and its strength estimated. The leaven hid in three measures of meal, however, working in a hidden way, affecting the very nature of all that it touches, represents the Kingdom as a moral and spiritual power, spreading its silent and unnoticed influence throughout human society. It depicts perfectly the effect of Christianity in a mission field such as China. It has a vast, pervasive influence on the ways of thinking, the standards of life of great numbers, an influence which cannot be expressed in statistics at all.

In both the parables it is the Kingdom as a social force which is uppermost in mind, though the comparisons are profoundly true of the Kingdom when considered as the rule of God in an individual life. Like a grain of mustard seed, God's rule in one's heart may spring from small beginnings; like the leaven, it will work pervasively throughout his whole nature until every aspect of life has been transformed by the truth, "every thought," in the words of Paul, having been brought "into captivity to the obedience of Christ." It is the kingdom of God in society, however, his reign in the world, which is principally in view in these two parables. We have already seen that in the two parables which follow these in the discourse of Jesus by the Sea of Galilee, the Pearl of Great Price and the Hidden Treasure, it is the rule of God as the supreme good in personal life which is emphasized. It is one Kingdom, in individual and social life. It is the rule of God, the enthronement of Jesus' ideal of character and life, in individuals and in society, in individuals first and then, through their influence and contacts, in society.

"THE WORLD THE SUBJECT OF REDEMPTION"

The best description of the kingdom of God is also the shortest. It occurs in the Lord's Prayer. "Thy kingdom come. Thy will be done, as in heaven so on earth." The kingdom of God on earth, for which we pray, hope, and labor, is the condition which prevails when God's will is done. A better translation of the phrase is "the reign of God." It is the pivotal idea of Jesus' teaching, so broad that he never gave a definition of it, and so all-inclusive that it is hard for us, who have been trained to think in terms of the individual, the family and the state, to grasp vividly so comprehensive an ideal. The reign of God is realized in a character which is dominated by a love like that of God. It is realized in society when the relations of men to men, of class to class, of nation to nation are controlled by that same love. Shailer Mathews expands this in his definition of it as "the joyous and righteous union of those who live as brothers with one another, because of their common faith in God as their Father, and their subjection to his rule of love." For us to believe in the Kingdom to-day means that we have faith that the rule of God and of love, which we see now only in its beginnings, will grow and expand until it embraces all peoples and all nations and will penetrate and transform their entire life. This is a vastly larger hope than that of simply saving a number of people out of the world and getting them into heaven. Men who have held such an interpretation of the plan of Christ regard the work of transforming the world as hopeless and not worth much effort. Those who have had such a view have often had a clear vision of Jesus' message of individual salvation and of eternal life. They have not understood as clearly his message for society and his purpose for the world. What is the social effect of a conception of Christianity which holds its purpose to be simply that of saving people out of the world into heaven? What light do these parables throw on such a view?

THE DIVINE METHOD OF GROWTH

These parables not only affirm the certainty of the Kingdom; they also point out the method of its coming. It is the method of gradual growth. As Jesus has expressed it in another parable (Mark 4. 28), "first the blade, then the ear, then the full grain in the ear." The development of the Kingdom comes under the great law of all development in nature, growth. From small and simple beginnings it expands slowly, steadily, surely. And therein lies the great hope. In this respect also the full force of these parables of Jesus has not always been felt or understood. Some have become so absorbed in the end of the world and in what is termed the second coming of Christ that they have overlooked this teaching of Jesus that the Kingdom grows as a tree grows and expands in power as leaven transforms dough. They have looked for the Kingdom to be ushered in suddenly by some great event from outside which would constitute the end of the world. Such a view has not infrequently an unfortunate tendency to decrease the willingness of its adherents to work for such measures of social betterment as take a long time to establish, as the abolition of war, of poverty and the liquor traffic, of industrial injustice. In its worst form this conception of the future of Christianity in the world is pessimistic in its outlook. It looks for the world to become worse and worse until it becomes so bad that God will end it. Surely, these parables point to a finer hope, a happier result.

THE LEAVEN AND HISTORY

Almost two thousand years have passed since Jesus spoke these parables. That is not enough to enable us to decide all the questions they raise. But it is enough for us to judge whether the actual facts of history bear out the faith of Jesus in the Kingdom's growth. Has the truth of Christ been like leaven in the world for twenty centuries? To ask the question is to answer it. The Christian religion has been incomparably the most powerful influence in all human history. Think of the parable of the leaven as applied to the history of Christianity. It is hard to conceive how any movement could be more effectually "hidden" than was the life and work of Jesus. It was a small movement among the obscure section of the despised population of a remote province of the Roman empire. Its leader died the death of a criminal. Its first leaders were hated by their own countrymen. It was limited almost entirely to the poor in the slums of the great cities and to the unlearned in small towns. It quickly drew upon itself ridicule and persecution. It had no rewards or honors to confer. Yet underneath the pomp and power of the Roman empire the ferment of Christian truth was working till Rome itself was gone and the leaven of Christ's kingdom had utterly transformed the world. The stone which the builders rejected has become the head of the corner. There is not a field of human endeavor and thought which has not been deeply affected by Christianity. Religion, ethics, philosophy, law, education, politics, literature, all have felt the transforming leaven of the influence of Christ. Architecture, music, literature, art "bear the marks of the Lord Jesus." How little anyone in the first two centuries dreamed of the mighty leaven hidden from view! How strikingly it shows that the street-corner test, the noise that a thing makes or the notice it attracts, is never the true test of the power or importance of a movement. The deeper we study the history of the Kingdom in the past the stronger faith we have in its future.

FORCES WHICH THE KINGDOM MUST CONQUER

The whole mass is not yet leavened. Vast tracts of life seem scarcely to have felt the pervasive influence of Christian truth. As we try to make our faith in the growth of the Kingdom vital and practical, we ask ourselves, "What must be overcome if it is to be victorious?" In general terms they are just the things which blocked the Kingdom in Jesus' own day, the things against which he had to wage incessant warfare—selfishness and covetousness, pride and hardness of heart, class and race prejudice, the oppression of the poor, externalism and legalism in religion. Their opposition is modern in form in some cases, but the root is the same. War and the selfish nationalism which lies behind it are still obstacles. The placing of material advantages above human and spiritual values; injustice and the exploitation of the workers in our system of industry; the waste and selfish extravagance of wealth; race prejudice, national prejudice, and class antipathy; divisions in the church; the active strength of non-Christian religions and the vast ignorance and traditionalism of the non-Christian world—these are a few of the enemies of the Kingdom which must be conquered. What others can you name? Which do you consider the strongest?

Forces in the Growing Kingdom

To estimate the forces which are evidence of the working
of the leaven of Christian truth would mean a survey of
the whole modern world. J. G. Greenough rightly warns
us against the mistake of taking only the parable of the
mustard seed and estimating the power of Christianity by
the number in the church and overlooking the mighty in-
vincible action of Christian influence and truth which act
as leaven. It is these forces, working frequently in an
invisible manner, which are the sure pledges of conquest.
Against the injustices of industry there must be set the
increasing recognition of the rights of labor, greater safeguards, better conditions; against the exploitation of women
and children in industry, set down the fact that protection
to them is being more rapidly extended than ever, and
that there was never so much intelligent care given to
childhood or such recognition of its value. Think of the
amazing restriction of the liquor traffic throughout the
world; the widespread horror of war, stronger than ever
before in history; the growing federation of the branches
of the church and the decrease of controversy; the new
emphasis of the church on social ministry; the wonders
of medical progress, the extension of education and of
democracy; the victory over such age-old curses as foot-
binding in China, and the voluntary abolition of the opium
trade; the advance in ethical standards in our own and
other nations in business and government; the break up
of many non-Christian religions—all these and a hundred
other results deepen our faith in the coming of the Kingdom.

The Challenge

The working of leaven implies contact with the meal
and that implication brings a direct challenge to us. The
Kingdom spreads *from* man *to* man and we must circulate
among our fellow men, bearing the leaven of a Christlike
life with us. We must touch life at all points so that its
religion, its labor, its recreation, its arts may be penetrated
with Christian ideals and standards. Dr. Plummer has
pointed out two mistakes which are commonly made and

which effectually hinder the spread of the Kingdom. One is keeping out of social contacts for fear of contamination. The other is to leave our Christianity behind when we go among men. How easy the latter is and how often we are tempted to do it! Think of the seriousness of such action, when the spread of the Kingdom depends on personal *Christian* contacts.

RELIGIOUS EDUCATION AND THE COMING KINGDOM

There are many methods of working to bring in the kingdom of God. "God fulfils himself in many ways." But there is one general field of work which deserves our particular thought, that of religious education. It deserves a special emphasis for two reasons; one, the part which it has played historically in the development and extension of the kingdom of God; the other, the fact that every one, no matter what his location, occupation, or situation, may fruitfully engage in it.

When we think of the relation of religious education to the growth of the Kingdom, our minds inevitably turn to Jesus and that little company of disciples, to whose intensive training he gave so lavishly of his time. While he did not neglect a public ministry to large crowds, he gave the largest part of his effort to the conduct of a teacher-training class. He indicated the supreme importance which he gave to religious education in the last command to his disciples, the command known as "the great commission," "Go ye therefore, and make disciples of all the nations, baptizing them in the name of the Father and of the Son and of the Holy Spirit: teaching them to observe all things whatsoever I commanded you" (Matt. 28. 19, 20).

When the early church confronted the Roman world with its opposing philosophies and religions, it prepared the way for its conquest of that world by the teaching of Christian doctrine by the church fathers, such as Origen, Tertullian, and Augustine. Again when, a few centuries later, Rome had broken down under the influx of barbarian hordes, the church preserved itself amid the general dissolution by the foundation of great schools, by which Christianity was spread among the conquerors of the Roman

empire. When the Reformation under Luther brought to
Europe a new and transforming knowledge of Christian
truth, that knowledge was extended and made fruitful by
a new emphasis on the teaching of the Bible and Christian
doctrine. One of the most effective agencies in the Methodist revival under Wesley was the class meeting, which
had an educational function in training new converts in
Christian truth and Christian living. It conserved and
made permanent the fruits of the great evangelistic movement. It is no exaggeration to say that the epochs in
which the Kingdom has had the greatest permanent growth
have been those in which the church has paid the most
attention to Paul's injunction to Timothy—"Give heed
. . . to teaching."

THE OPPORTUNITY OF RELIGIOUS EDUCATION TO-DAY

Never was there a greater opportunity for the extension
of the Kingdom through education in religion than to-day.
To a degree scarcely ever before realized the world is making a fresh start, beginning a new epoch. Abroad, in non-
Christian lands, the breaking up of old established ways of
thought and customs presents an unparalleled opportunity
of teaching Christianity. "One quarter of the human race
is slipping from its spiritual moorings. Surely never was
richer freight derelict on the waters of time." The effect
of Christian education in China, for instance, can readily
be seen in the fact that a large number of the leaders in
her progress in the last ten years were educated in Christian
mission schools. At home the opportunity is equally
strategic. To give to the next generation Christian ideals
of personal conduct, of home life, of business and industrial
relations, and of international comity, is the largest task to
which we can give ourselves.

We are often discouraged at the slow moral and spiritual
progress the world seems to make. But hope for the Kingdom gleams bright when we remember that there is a new
generation on earth every thirty years. If we only do our
part with fidelity and thoroughness, some time there will
be a generation on earth which has been trained rightly,
and then the progress of the Kingdom will literally go

forward by a leap of centuries. Is your church meeting this challenge and opportunity of religious education in the community to which it ministers?

For Reflection and Discussion

What is the place of religious education in the growth of the Kingdom?

In what respects has there been a higher standard of ethics within the last twenty-five years in business practices? In political life?

How does our treatment of the dependent classes, such as the sick, the poor, the crippled, the defective, compare with a generation ago?

How would you answer the statement that the Great War had shown the breakdown of Christianity?

In what ways is the missionary enterprise hopeful to-day? What are its chief obstacles? Are all the obstacles on the foreign field?

How does hope for the Kingdom embrace the great national and social aspirations of to-day?

What form of government seems to you best adapted to the promotion of the ideals of Jesus?

Do you believe the Sermon on the Mount, properly interpreted, could be made dominant in our social life? What sacrifices would it mean for different classes in the community, such as employers and employees?

Are we as a nation making progress toward the ideal of Christian brotherhood? What evidences do you find for your answer?

How do you account for the fact that the best movements so often become debased?

Would Christianity be just as influential as a social power of salvation if the church did not exist?

CHAPTER XIII

THE LAST JUDGMENT

Matthew 25. 31-46

"When the Son of man comes in his glory and *all the angels with him*, then he will sit on the throne of his glory, and all nations will be gathered in front of him; he will separate them one from another, as a shepherd separates the sheep from the goats, setting the sheep on his right hand and the goats on his left. Then shall the King say to those on his right, 'Come, you whom my Father has blessed, come into your inheritance in the realm prepared for you from the foundation of the world.

For I was hungry and you fed me,
I was thirsty and you gave me drink,
I was a stranger and you entertained me,
I was unclothed and you clothed me,
I was ill and you looked after me,
I was in prison and you visited me.'

Then the just will answer,
'Lord, when did we see you hungry and fed you? or thirsty and gave you drink?
when did we see you a stranger and entertain you? or unclothed and clothed you?
when did we see you ill or in prison and visit you?'

The King will answer them, 'I tell you truly, in so far as you did it to one of these brothers of mine, even to the least of them, you did it to me.' Then he will say to those on the left, 'Begone from me, you accursed ones, to the eternal fire which has been prepared for the devil and his angels!

For I was hungry but you never fed me,
I was thirsty but you never gave me drink,
I was a stranger but you never entertained me,
I was unclothed but you never clothed me,
I was ill and in prison but you never looked after me.'

Then they will answer too, 'Lord, when did we ever see you hungry or thirsty or a stranger or unclothed or ill or in prison, and did not minister to you?' Then he will answer them, 'I tell you truly, in so far as you did not do it to one of these, even the least of them, you did not do it to me.'

So they shall depart to eternal punishment,
and the just to eternal life."

The Final Separation

The good man, in an age of savagery, was the strong man. The aristocrat was the one who could deal the stoutest blow or swing the heaviest club. The first test of human value was physical. Men have also been judged as good or worthless according to race. The Greek expressed his sense of superiority by dividing all men into Greeks and Barbarians. The Hebrew did the same with his terms "Jew" and "Gentile." This crude type of classification is still kept alive by race prejudice. Another common basis for estimating worth to-day is wealth. Frequently it is social standing and family connection by which men are classified; frequently it is an intellectual test—separating the learned from the ignorant. Sometimes it is religious, men being rated good or bad according to whether they are members of the church or not.

In view of these varied classifications Jesus' division of mankind into two great classes is intensely interesting. There is a deep solemnity in his announcement that it is the final separation and the only one that has eternal significance. He passes by every time-honored standard of value which has ever been applied. His basis of judgment is not intellectual, financial, or even religious, in the conventional sense. Men are to be judged simply on the basis of whether or not they have shown love to their fellows. For that determines their true relationship to Him. No matter what intellectual achievements may be ours, no matter how high our social position or how honored our name, no matter how perfect our record of religious observances, if we have walked through life with eyes blinded by selfishness or indifference, if we have lived in the presence of suffering and hunger and loneliness and oppression and have not been stirred to minister to their relief, we have no place in the eternal kingdom of God, and are cast out into darkness. Surely, these are the most solemn words ever pronounced!

The Aristocracy of God

Think what an overturning this picture makes of the

ideas of goodness and acceptance with God which were common among the Jews of Jesus' day. Is it any the less upsetting to the common ideas of goodness in our time? It reveals a vast difference between the divine estimate of human goodness and worth and the human estimate. It is a vivid New Testament illustration of the Old Testament declaration, "For my thoughts are not your thoughts, neither are your ways my ways, saith Jehovah. For as the heavens are higher than the earth, so are my ways higher than your ways" (Isa. 55. 8, 9). The surprising feature of the judgment, both to those who were admitted to the Kingdom and to those who were shut out, was that Christ claimed the poor and needy as his brethren in so real a sense that what was done to them was done to him. But such a claim is in keeping with his character as the Son of man and Son of God. God is his Father and their Father. It is a realistic portrayal of the truth that to love God is to love man, and to serve God is to serve man.

How many of the tests of goodness and worth which we commonly apply to ourselves and others Jesus utterly rules out! There is no mention of creeds. Yet think how widespread has been the belief that correct ideas about religious doctrine would fit a man for the final judgment. Those who were shut out were no doubt every bit as orthodox in their opinions as the others, perhaps some of them more so. Yet correctness of opinion, if it is barren of the good fruit of mercy and love, is of no value at God's judgment, however high it may be rated in lower courts.

Religious connections are likewise valued at zero. People get into the unconscious habit of thinking that familiarity with ecclesiastical affairs and mingling with religious people, or holding some religious position, in some way becomes automatically a virtue in them. The delusion is helped on by the fact that it does secure recognition for them on earth.

Wealth and reputation likewise are "counted unto men for righteousness" in earthly courts. Unfortunately, Saint James' warning against respect of persons is frequently a description of actual happening. "For if there come into your synagogue a man with a gold ring, in fine clothing, and there come in also a poor man in vile clothing; and ye have regard to him that weareth the fine clothing, and say, Sit thou here in a good place; and ye say to the poor man, Stand thou there, or sit under my footstool; do ye not make distinctions among yourselves, and become judges with evil thoughts?" (James 2. 2-4.) But the court of the last judgment is a bankruptcy court so far as earthly wealth is concerned. What value would a complete command of the French language be to us if the examination we had to stand were on mathematics? Just as much value as learning, wealth, power, with or without religious connections, will be when God will judge us on the basis of something entirely different, our attitude toward men and the reality of our neighborliness.

"IF—"

Mr. Gladstone was once asked what his wish would be, if he could have one wish granted. He replied that it would be that men's beliefs might become their convictions. What a difference it would make in the world if the belief of all Christian people that love to their fellow men is a beautiful quality, should become an intense conviction that the amount of ministering love they showed their fellow men would be the sole determining factor in their eternal destiny! Think of the changes such a conviction would bring. Would there be quite so much unrelieved poverty? Quite so many suicides? Quite so many babies dying for lack of pure milk and proper care? Would there be so many children in orphan asylums, with so many childless homes? Would only a fraction of one per cent of the population have any idea what the county jail was like, or how the town farm was conducted? Would there be quite so many saloons to keep the jail and poorfarm filled? Would there be as many automobiles bought every year as there are now? Think over your own life for the past year. What difference would such an intense conviction make in it?

"WHEN SAW WE THEE HUNGRY?"

To order our life with a clear appreciation of the basis

of the last judgment means that we bring into it both a new motive and a new scale of values. The new motive which dignifies and exalts even the lowliest service is the knowledge that it is acceptable as an offering to Christ himself. The new scale of values will rate as of the highest importance every opportunity of service. The things which we have rejected in the building of our careers, the personal consultations which we grudged because they took time from business, the visits to sick friends which were depressing, the committee meeting, the Sunday school class, the calls of poor relatives, and old time friends who were always in hard luck become vastly important. Weighed by Christ's standard these are the most important things we do.

It is well to remember that the love which wins the welcome "Come, ye blessed of my Father, inherit the kingdom," is a love which goes out of its way to find the stranger, the sick, the unclothed, and the prisoner. It is rather easy to "brighten the corner where you are." The fundamental Christian message is to brighten the corner where some one else is and which you go out of your beaten path to find. "The Son of man came to seek and to save." Most of us are willing to help to save some one who may happen to need saving at a place conveniently near to us. Where we fail to follow Christ is in seeking those who need saving. The stranger, the naked, the sick, the prisoner—all these represent classes that we must go out of our way to find. What kind of excuse would it be for not visiting those in prison to say that we never saw any prisoners? How could we expect to see any, in our office or at church or on the boulevard? It has been truly said that if people could actually see the misery within ten blocks of them, they could not eat their dinner in peace. The Christian conscience must annihilate those ten blocks and spoil the dinner! We eat too many dinners in peace anyhow. When Richard Watson Gilder was on the Tenement House Commission of New York he wanted to find out the cause of the many tenement house fires. He had a fire department gong placed in his bedroom and every tenement house fire was reported on the gong, so that he might go. He went out of his way to serve. His love was so great that he allowed himself to be riotously disturbed by the needs of others. That gong connecting his home with the lower East Side is a fit symbol of the Christian love which this parable demands. How wide a circle does your daily work cover? How much actual need do you see every day? How much do you know about that which you do not see?

MINISTRY BY PREVENTION

In our complex life to-day a very merciful form of ministry is loving and effective prevention. It is frequently not so spectacular a way of showing love, but it yields far larger returns in social benefit and blessing. Let us visit the prisoners and do all in our power to see that they are ministered to with true humanity. But by putting the saloon out of business there will not be nearly so many prisoners to suffer. We minister to the sick both by the kindly visit to those afflicted and by the energetic endeavor to change conditions which cause sickness. We clothe the naked both by a gift of clothing and by a vigorous help to all the forces which are working for a fairer distribution of the profits of industry, so that men shall be more able to clothe their own families.

"BEFORE HIM SHALL BE GATHERED ALL NATIONS"

But can we limit this love to our own town or even nation? The vast increase in the facilities of communication and travel have made the world very much smaller. Joseph Cook once said: "The nineteenth century has made the world a neighborhood. The twentieth century will make it a brotherhood." The twentieth century *must* make it a brotherhood, for the fact that the telegraph, wireless, steamship, and railroad have brought the world to our very door has vastly increased our responsibility to minister to its need. The Orient has been moved into our back yard. We can go to Japan in the time which it took to go from Baltimore to Boston by stage during the Revolution. As the Orient grows nearer in time and accessibility, our responsibility deepens. The work of the Y. M. C. A. of America in ministering to the six million men in European prison camps during the war is an illustration of the modern meaning of "I was in prison, and ye came unto me." Will it be a valid excuse for us in the Day of Judgment to say that we never saw any starving Armenians, or orphaned Belgians, or hungry Chinamen, or desolate children in India?

"YE HAVE DONE IT UNTO ME"

It must never be imagined that this parable teaches that philanthropy can take the place of religion or that if a man is kind and generous, he has no need of religion. It joins religion to conduct in the most thoroughgoing way, for it supplies the strongest motive to service to our fellow men which has ever been conceived. It shows that service to man is service to God, and puts the high and strong incentive of devotion to Christ into all deeds of mercy and love. The parable assigns the highest possible place in men's lives to religion, for it makes a man's entrance into the Kingdom depend on his relation to Christ. The genuineness of that relation to Christ is evidenced in turn by their conduct toward their fellow men. Out of the motive of devotion to Christ which is pictured here has flowed the great stream of Christian benevolence, social feeling, and practical helpfulness. "The streams that turn the machinery of the world take their rise in solitary places." In the motive of devotion to Christ a vast amount of the energy for the tasks of social service has taken its rise. Tennyson, in his poem, "In the Children's Hospital," has shown the spiritual energy which this very parable supplies for the work of ministry to need. A little girl is being prepared for a surgical operation and prays to Jesus to help her bear the pain and the skeptical surgeon smiles half in contempt at her faith. Then the nurse who tells the story adds:

"Then he muttered half to himself, but I know that I heard
    him say,
'All very well—but the good Lord Jesus has had his day.'

"Had? has it come? It has only dawned. It will come by and
   by.
O how could I serve in the wards if the hope of the world
   were a lie?
How could I bear with the sights and the loathsome smells
   of disease
But that He said, 'Ye do it to me, when ye do it to these'?"

THE WARNING

The parable raises the startling thought of what a perfectly respectable, upright, and honored life a man may
lead and yet miss completely entrance into the Kingdom!
That was the great surprise of the judgment to those who
were cast out into darkness, and they were struck with
utter consternation. Their first wild thought was that
they had been mistaken for some one else, that they had
never neglected Christ. Have we unconsciously fallen into
the habit of allowing man's approval to take the place of
the eager quest of God's approval? Think of the surprise
awaiting a man well regarded in his city, one of its substantial citizens, of high personal character, the father of
a fine family who were members of the church; an upright
man but a busy man who had no time to be "bothered"
with beggars and collections and charity and reform movements; who "didn't believe in foreign missions"—think
of his surprise to learn that his high position of respect in
his community, his irreproachable social and family connections, had no weight whatever in the Last Judgment.
Does not such a picture cause us to pause and examine the
proportion of time and effort *we* give to the only things
that are going to count after all? A question which was
often on the lips of Martin Luther deserves attention from
all of us, "What will God Almighty say about it in the
end?"

FOR REFLECTION AND DISCUSSION

What means of religious education can be used to impress
   the emphasis which Jesus placed upon love and service?
   Why has this emphasis of Jesus so frequently been lost
   sight of?
What forces have been active in the social awakening of the

church in the present day? What is the place of the religious motive in social service? Is it to-day a strong or a weak one?

What kinds of need are there in a city which we do not see unless we look for them? In a country community?

In what respects is the spirit of Jesus manifested in your community in its relation to dependent and delinquent children?

In what different ways does war oppose the Christian principle of love?

Is your religious life occupied with secondary or primary interests?

What activities can a Bible class or Sunday school carry on which correspond to the things commended by Jesus?

25

Lu

St

DATE DUE			
FEB 12 '01			
FEB 15 02			
FEB 8 02			
JAN 19 03			
12/15/03			
1/5/04			
1/15/04			

The Library Store #47-0204